SPORTS WEIRD-O-PEDIA

The Ultimate Book of Surprising, Strange, and Incredibly Bizarre Facts about Sports

LEW FREEDMAN

Racehorse Publishing

Cover design by Daniel Brount
Cover illustrations by iStockphoto

Print ISBN: 978-1-5107-5445-4

Printed in China

contents

INTRODUCTION

S ports achievements have the capacity to inspire and excite watchers, whether through athletic brilliance or magnificent team performance. Sports fans root hard for their favorite individuals and clubs, building strong allegiances.

———

Championship victories can spread joy across a city, state, region, even a nation. We may be enthralled by the rare or unique play when the seemingly impossible becomes reality, but sometimes we are reminded that games are merely games and the players are all-too-human. There are times our athletes and teams go wacko on us, and the most peculiar things break out with no warning to provide wide-eyed astonishment, or laugh-out-loud responses. Those spontaneous combustions can be memorable.

While those occasions may result from someone rising from the weird side of the bed, there are also actual sports competitions that are so far out there it may take a little open-mindedness to even classify them as sports. They provide built-in weirdness.

Sometimes this built-in weirdness merely stems from cultural differences, as in what may be a big deal in Scandinavia may not be a big deal in Cleveland. Other times, by any standard of normal behavior, a performance or event cannot escape the definition of weirdness.

—Lew Freedman

CHAPTER 1
WEIRD SPORTS

WIFE CARRYING

We have all heard of the newlywed tradition of carrying a wife across the threshold of the house following a wedding, but in Finland, picking up the Mrs. and carrying her a much longer distance is popular sport.

—

Wife carrying originated in that Scandinavian country, perhaps in the 800s, though that is murky. Back then, it was called kidnapping when bad men raided villages and stole food and carried off local women. Apparently not every sport has a proud (or legal) origin.

—

More recently, wife carrying has gained an aura of respectability in the form of an annual world championship contest in Sonkajarvi, Finland. Men throw women over their shoulders and try to run through an 831.7-foot obstacle course as fast as possible. Rather than being derided as criminals, as occurred in the old days, the men are feted like kings, or at least drunkards. First prize is the wife's weight in beer.

> "While the sport is still referred to as wife carrying, apparently rules have loosened up sufficiently so that contestants must only be a him and a her, regardless of wedding bands being involved or not, though they must be at least 17 years of age."

Just how a dude carries his "wife" along the course is up to him. Experiments in form efficiency have varied from the piggyback ride to the woman hanging upside down and backward on the man's shoulders, with head and torso draped over his back while wrapping her arms around his waist, labeled Estonian style. That's guaranteed to leave the Miss or Mrs. dizzy.

While definitely not for everyone, the "sport" has caught on selectively in other locations, including Estonia, but also in Australia, the United States, England, India, and Hong Kong. While the North

American championships take place in Maine, other hotbeds of US wife carrying can be found in Minnesota, Michigan, and Wisconsin.

———

In at least a single race in England, the roles were reversed, with the woman carrying the man. And once in Finland, a male contender carried another male in drag who stood 7-foot-4 and weighed 308 pounds.

COMPETITIVE EATING

In a world where serious-minded, concerned people say 1 in 9 people go to bed hungry and 34 million children suffer from severe malnutrition, it can easily be argued that the existence of competitive eating as a sport is unseemly. But if anyone can figure out a way to instantly transport the hot dogs devoured on July 4 directly from Coney Island, New York, to Niger, Sudan, or Zambia, they should email the State Department.

———

If conscience is removed from the equation, many aspects of competitive eating, not only in the flagship event, but as mere slapstick site gags and digestion of statistics, can be viewed as super weird. While no doubt aspects of competitive eating can be construed as being in bad taste, a temporary willing suspension of concern for those less fortunate may leave the observer open to laughs and certainly to disbelief.

George Shea, commissioner of Major League Eating, is a gifted gabber who can rattle off one-liners with the speed of a Gatling gun. In his distinctive straw boater, he is the epitome of a huckster from years gone by, but very much a funny man, as well. As the July 4 master of ceremonies on the boardwalk at Coney Island, Shea is the front man for the all-you-can-eat competition.

The entire deal is weird, but it can also be pretty darned humorous when Shea twists the language to his advantage, uttering a comment about a contestant being "the Evel Knievel of the alimentary canal" because he escaped from being buried in popcorn by eating his way through the pile.

Competitive eating counts volume and measures speed, as in how many hot dogs did Joey Chestnut eat in 2018? The man nicknamed "Jaws" devoured 74, with buns, in 10 minutes, an event record. He was presented with a mustard-colored championship belt. There once was a popular TV commercial about hamburgers asking, "Where's the beef?" Apparently, it is all in Chestnut's stomach.

It should be noted that the holiday hot-dog contest dates back to July 4, 1916, founded as an advertising gimmick. Only in recent years after the Major League Eating organization was formed has the contest received attention and TV exposure.

The countdown to the eat-off resembles a heavyweight title fight, albeit with many more than 2 combatants poised to enter the ring. The devourers' credentials are read aloud, just as if they were being recited from the back of a baseball card. For those on a diet whose hands accidentally paused on the clicker while looking for another show, and who never knew such things existed, being grossed out by some accomplishments may come with the territory.

> Chestnut alone has eaten 47 grilled cheese sandwiches in 10 minutes, 390 shrimp wantons in 8 minutes, 141 hard boiled eggs in 8 minutes, and 121 Twinkies in 6 minutes.

Eric "Badlands" Booker, a former 365-pound NFL player, has eaten 49 glazed doughnuts in 8 minutes and 2 pounds of chocolate bars in 6 minutes. According to another guy's résumé, he consumed 47 ears of sweet corn, and someone else downed 170 chicken wings—on the clock. There must have been a whole lot of burping going on.

CHEESE ROLLING

Eating grilled cheese appeals to those of all ages. Putting cheese on a burger to turn it into a cheeseburger is a common practice. And the most popular sandwich in Philadelphia is the legendary cheese steak.

———

However, it is a lock that few Americans have heard of the sport of cheese rolling. Clearly, the main implement must be shaped differently from much of the cheese people devour. Cheese Whiz comes in a can. Tiny pieces of cheese are often mixed into Caesar salads. But for cheese rolling competitions, something more substantial in size is required.

———

Cheese rolling is quite popular in a place called Gloucestershire, England. It is not a team sport, but an individual pursuit. The event is called Cooper's Hill Cheese Rolling, the name applied because of the location.

———

Once a year (something to look forward to), large cheese wheels are rolled out. Perched upon a very steep hill, the wheel is set loose to roll down the hill, picking up speed, as a crowd of humans gives chase. The first person to make it to the bottom of the hill earns first place and first prize. Naturally enough, the reward for first place is the cheese itself.

Initially an entirely local event scheduled for Spring Bank Holiday (the last Monday in May), cheese rolling caught enough of the world's attention for people from other countries to visit the town to compete, although it does not seem to have caught quite enough of the world's attention that widespread knowledge of the event is out there on the tip of everyone's tongue in, say, Ghana.

> While many in the region believe the tradition dates back even earlier, the semiofficial origin of cheese rolling is given as 1826.

Encased in wood, the cheese weighs 9 pounds and is rolled off the top of the hill with a 1-second head start in front of the humans massed behind it. Turns out cheese so wrapped has the balance and staying power of a tire, and the wheel has been known to reach speeds of 70 mph. After the cheese caused some injuries due to the weight of the object, coupled with the speed attained, a substitute cheese made of foam assumed the role of being chased. Still, the winner is awarded real-deal cheese.

As more and more people turn out for a shot at the cheese, the 1-race cheese roll has been separated into categories, including a women's division. Most recently, there have been as many as 5 cheese-chasing competitions on race day.

> Likely, winners respond to the command of "Say cheese" when having their pictures snapped.

EXTREME IRONING

The old television show *Wide World of Sports* was known for introducing viewers to sports activities that were considered out of the mainstream, far removed from such well-known competitions as baseball, football, and boxing.

But even *Wide World of Sports* likely would have kept its distance from Extreme Ironing. For 1 thing, nobody would believe such an event existed; and for the other, taking a step back, the suspense and action of running a hot iron over a pair of pants to eliminate wrinkles does not seem to get the juices going.

—

Yes, there is such a thing as Extreme Ironing. Whether more than a dozen people in the world would call it sport is another thing altogether. "Athletes" are required to tote ironing boards to remote places, whip out an iron, and smooth articles of clothing.

—

Every sport must have a governing body (being consistent with the Olympic model and all that), and the Extreme Ironing Bureau proclaimed itself "the latest danger sport that combines the thrills of an extreme outdoor activity with the satisfaction of a well-pressed shirt." But of course.

—

Events like this often are created when a bunch of friends with a sense of humor are sitting together in a bar till closing time and they are on their 12th beer and issue ever-more outrageous challenges. One might surmise. However, this is not how Extreme Ironing was jump-started. Extreme Ironing origins are as easy to trace as the origins of basketball and the legendary Dr. James Naismith inventing his YMCA game.

—

Credit for the birth of Extreme Ironing goes to an Englishman named Tony Hiam. In 1980, Hiam observed that his brother-in-law was such a neat freak that he even ironed his clothing in a tent on a camping trip. Trying to prove to his relative this was absurd behavior, Hiam began ironing clothing in airports and on top of telephone booths, and invading charity clothing collections and straightening them up. A movement was born, though basically all about making fun.

> It was not until somewhat later a fellow named Phil Shaw took ironing to new extremes. Pressed for time when he wanted to go rock climbing in 1997 yet also feeling the obligation to keep up appearances, 1 day in the interests of time efficiency, Shaw took his ironing into the wilderness. Voilà! A 2-for-1 time savings.

Once was not enough for Shaw. He actually saw a potential new sport in his outing. After that, it might be said things began sizzling. Shaw traveled to several countries promoting Extreme Ironing, and while certainly many deemed him a lunatic (particularly women who felt the assignment was more drudgery than competition), those with amusement in their souls began trying to 1-up others by seeking out the most extreme and ridiculous places to carry along their ironing.

Thus, with only a limit on imagination, Extreme Ironing has taken place high above cliffs, in canoes, on highways, on top of a tree, and even underwater. Also, somewhat stunningly, a wardrobe was ironed slightly above Mount Everest Base Camp at about 20,000 feet of altitude.

> Twelve teams from 10 countries competed in the 1st Extreme Ironing Championships in 2002 in Germany.

A top-notch competitor nicknamed "Steam" dreamed up a new way to iron on the fly. While running a half-marathon in England in 2012, this gentleman strapped an ironing board to his back, and, performing double duty, he periodically paused during the run to iron clothing. The approach did not do much for his finishing time, but he did have fresh clothes to change into when done.

TOE WRESTLING

Neatly following the pattern of just what can emerge from a skull session when spirits run freely through the bloodstream, the invention of toe wrestling really did stem from some guys sitting around a tavern letting their tongues wag freely.

Sure enough, this occasion also took place in England, birthplace of both cheese rolling and Extreme Ironing. Out for a convivial visit to a pub in Staffordshire in 1974, this gang of 4 had no idea it was poised to make history. A foursome of friends, perhaps thinking back to their schoolboy history lessons when the British Empire stretched from sea to sea, complained how their favorite country never won world sporting championships anymore.

They set about creating a sport they hoped could make Great Britain great once again. Hence, toe wrestling. Next to trying to outrun the guy next door, wrestling is probably the oldest sport known to mankind.

> So why not toe wrestling? From the start, it appeared minimal equipment would be necessary. And unlike some other sports where innocent observers might say, "Are you crazy? You could get killed doing that!" toe wrestling seemed fairly safe from serious injury.

The fundamentals of the sport are stripping off shoes and socks to reveal naked feet as the implements of destruction. In the world of professional boxing, a second, or handler, often observes the taping of an opponent's hands before he inserts them into padded gloves. In toe wrestling, the opponents generally take off the foes' shoes and socks for him.

The starting position for a match has players sitting down. The legs are outstretched, right foot extended, and then placed flat against the opponent's right foot. Toes are linked. Players have 3 seconds to pin the other's foot. Don't blink. In the 2nd round of the best 2-out-of-3, the left feet are used. Then, it is back to the right feet.

———

An annual world championship is conducted, but nobody is holding their breath waiting for the International Olympic Committee to designate toe wrestling as an Olympic sport.

NAKI SUMO

Since so few Americans speak fluent Japanese, the words "Naki Sumo" may at first blush sound as if they could be describing something in the alcoholic beverage family like saki. But no. The translation of Naki Sumo into English represents a sport apparently confined to the island of Japan: competitive baby crying.

———

While this showdown seems as if it should be conducted on an airplane, since that's what seems to happen every time you board a flight, in reality jets are not the playing fields for these events. Rather, the sport is contested at a Crying Baby Festival. The king of Crying Baby Festivals takes place in Tokyo, but there are others of lesser prestige. Overall, this sport offers a new definition of tag-team wrestling.

———

Under the rules, 2 sumo wrestlers attired in their usual diaper-like outfits and nothing more hold the little ones and pit the babies against each other to see who can cry the longest. One basic criterion is the babies must be born within the previous year. The setting is actually a sumo ring, and the protagonists stand opposite each other holding up the children. Then, each gigantic sumo man tries to scare the other's kid into crying.

> Parents vie for the chance to have their baby so displayed and can pay entry fees of 10,000 yen or more to get into the mix. It is not known if anyone has ever suggested that the babies wrestle and the sumo wrestlers be cajoled into crying.

If the babies are of such strong character that a sumo wrestler can't provoke them into crying, the referee steps in, puts on a scary mask, and takes a crack at making them cry. Unlike the National Basketball Association in the United States, which did not get its start until 1946 but is known for its whining about foul calls, Naki Sumo competition dates back about 400 years.

The origin of this activity stems from a proverb that says a crying baby will thrive. It is also said the ritual is a prayer for the baby's healthy growth. One catchphrase associated with the event is "Crying babies grow fat," though it is not clear if those words appear on bumper stickers.

Of course, the healthy and happy parts don't kick in until the baby gets over the trauma of being frightened by a giant. There is uncertainty about this because postgame interviews with the babies are limited, since they cannot yet talk. After the confrontation, probably all of the adults get together for some saki.

LOG ROLLING

In Wisconsin and the upper Midwest of the United States or other timber productive areas, people might take offense at the notion log rolling classifies as a weird sport, but supporters of baby crying festivals would probably think so if they watched 2 people climb upon a log floating in a body of water, stand up straight, and then attempt to spin the log as fast as they can until either of them splashes down.

There is a particular set of skills associated with log rolling, from very good balance to quick feet, in addition to a willingness to get wet if there are any defeats in a best 2-out-of-3 competition.

"Log rolling is a staple at the annual Lumberjack World Championships in Hayward, Wisconsin, a gathering of athletic wood choppers and others who excel at timber sports."

A United States Logrolling Association dictates the rules of the game, but logs are approximately 13 feet long and between 12 and 15 inches in diameter, depending on the professional and amateur categories. Besides being the governing body of this activity, the association also supervises boom running. Boom running involves sprinting over floating logs without tumbling into the water.

The origins of log rolling date to the 1800s and are an offshoot of the type of work lumberjacks did when logs jammed up on bodies of water. Men jumped aboard to move them along downriver. Ultimately, challenges were issued in lumber camps to see who was the best or fastest at log rolling and other tasks. This caught on, and championships were organized, logging companies forming teams. The first known log rolling championship took place in 1898.

> Many timber-sport events require brute strength, and the competitors are football lineman—sized. Not so in log rolling, where the entries are typically slightly built, more resembling long-distance runners, though with faster feet.

Unlike some other timber activities where sharp blades are required, kids do try this at home and get their start in log rolling at young ages. Indeed, in 2018, a child named Libby Lu appeared on the American TV show *Little Big Shots* hosted by Steve Harvey, showing off her log rolling skills.

GURNING

It's doubtful 1-in-100,000 Americans have heard of gurning, a sport that calls for making funny faces. And about the same number may classify it as a sport. But if that's what is going through the mind, those people should be careful about insulting gurning around their English friends. Gurning is another United Kingdom invention, at least as competition, as opposed to everyday life.

———

Funny faces, grimaces, and extreme facial muscle movement come under the heading of gurning. Competitions of the sort date back at least to 1267, a time when it might be said there was a premium on recreational opportunities, especially in rural village areas that did not get first-run movies. Some of those places may even have Internet access these days, but that doesn't mean they let the tradition of rubbery-faced posing cease. Naturally, there is a world championship, and it takes place annually at the Egremont Crab Fair.

———

At its simplest explanation, gurning is the equivalent of just making a face, something you got into trouble for doing in the 3rd grade when you thought the teacher wasn't looking. There is no seriousness involved in this sport. People contort their facial muscles every which way, twisting their mouths, raising their eyebrows, wiggling their ears. In a sense, this is lowest-common-denominator humor, most often practiced by children and those who never quite grew up.

Muscular flexibility appears to be the key to success, demonstrating a variety of tricks with the upper and lower lips. When it comes to competition, some people, apparently viewing their facial performances as works of art, began using horse collars to frame them as if they were paintings. Maybe this is the ultimate selfie.

Beauty being in the eye of the beholder, it is said that those who have no teeth have an advantage because that offers more freedom to manipulate the jaw. One contender actually had his teeth removed to aid his ability to make more extreme faces in competition. Left unsaid is how those people cope the other 364 days of the year.

> A woman named Anne Woods, who died in 2015, won the women's division 28 times, making her the queen of gurning.

BATHTUB RACING

Instead of putting your body into the bathtub to wash, this event requires you to transplant your bathtub outdoors and into the Pacific Ocean, followed by you climbing in and revving up a motor.

—

Bathtub racing—the bathtubs are not the same superheavy models you might find in the house, but in many cases are hot-rod modified, so to speak—was introduced to the world in 1967 in Nanaimo, British Columbia, on Vancouver Island by then-mayor Frank Ney, an unabashed promoter of his community.

—

On the 100th anniversary of the founding of the city, something special was called for to commemorate the occasion, and Ney thought of it. Everyone wants to get noticed and be loved, and Ney felt that way about his city, placing the potential for long-term good, attention, and tourism ahead of any early ridicule.

—

Some 200 tubbers entered the 36-mile race when the "Nanaimo To Vancouver Great International World Bathtub Race" made its debut. Interest was obviously present from the beginning. There were many fewer rules and a greater variety of tubs.

—

What can we say? The man was right, and the annual July race continues past its 50th anniversary. The race has long outlasted

Ney, who passed away in 1992, with a terrific legacy attached to his name. Ney never tired of promoting his baby and dressed as a pirate before casting off in his own vessel. These days, there is a statue of him on the dock.

—

As might be expected by inventors with itchy trigger fingers living in a high-tech world, bathtub development has matured over the years. There is more than a single class of boat for racing nowadays, with divisions based on motor power. Each tub must weigh at least 350 pounds. One might think at that weight the pass-as-a-boat-for-a-day tub would sink. The rules are more sophisticated than originally contemplated, but nothing ever stays the same in this world. Some bathtubs are decorated with the same flair as Indianapolis 500 cars.

—

It cannot be said bathtub racing has taken the sports world by storm (and storms are to be avoided on the seas), but there are other such races in Washington State, just across the Canadian border, and in New Zealand. Still room for growth elsewhere.

—

Meanwhile, the bathtub retains a certain special cachet in Nanaimo. From the start, the city has expressed a fondness for "the spirit of tubbing."

CAMEL WRESTLING

While animal rights organizations oppose hunting, fishing, the circus, rodeo, dogsled racing, or camel wrestling, their angst is never likely to be soothed. That's because they can't count on having the same effect on event sponsors as they do in the United States.

> Camel wrestling is not a big-city US thing, not nearly as popular a sport as long-distance running, or auto racing on July 4 or Labor Day. However, Tulu camel wrestling has been going on in Turkey for something like 2,400 years.

Although humans have injected themselves into organizing camel wrestling competitions, the rules of the game are very similar to what occurs in the wild amongst other species. Basically, the strong survive.

The toughest, most attractive male bear mates with a female grizzly. Moose and elk have mating seasons. Get it? Camels also have seasonally adjusted mating times. Left alone without human interference, two big, strong male camels could well fight it out over the charms of a female camel crossing their paths. A female camel in heat is led in front of 2 male camels to arouse their attention, and to simply arouse them. The lady camel is the bait, and once the male camels figure out it's me or him, they fight it out, using their necks as the primary implements of force. A match is declared over when 1 camel is hurled to the ground.

> Wrestling camels are prized animals, also coming with price tags of $20,000. That's a pretty big deal when the average annual household income in Turkey was $3,800 in 2016.

Camel wrestling is a popular sport in sections of Turkey, usually in the most rural of areas. Most camel wrestling is conducted at

festivals on Sundays. Matches can run for 10 minutes, but a fighting festival includes several showdowns on the program, much like
a boxing card that may have 8 or 10 bouts on it on a given night.

There is no shortage of camel combat action during a festival where sometimes as many as 100 camels are brought to town.
Interestingly, there is no prize money offered to winners. The payoff
is pretty much my-camel-is-tougher-than-your-camel boasting.

Although around for 24 centuries, camel wrestling fell out of
favor for a while in the 20th century but is experiencing a resur-
gence as part of a cultural renaissance. In fact, there are now some
camel beauty pageants taking place in Turkey. Turkey remains the
hotbed of camel wrestling, but a few other countries have dabbled
in the sport. It hasn't made it to the US yet, though.

SHIN KICKING

Is this boxing with the feet? Is it a toddler tantrum with more
damage?

Those feisty Englishmen have been dreaming up extreme con-
tests for centuries, and this contest is a doozy. Shin kicking has been
part of the national psyche since the 1600s and somehow perseveres
today as a martial arts-type event designed to inflict pain and suffering. It is soccer without the ball, or many rules, either.

> Although shin kicking is what it is, some British subjects employ synonyms for the sport, "hacking" and "purring" being other choices. Purring seems to be a misnomer. Maybe "screaming."

Under whatever name, "Ouch" may be the operative word in this sport. Actually, as it turns out, that's not quite true. In the United States some years back, the verbal signal that a fighter had taken enough punishment was expelling the word *uncle*. When someone gives up in a shin-kicking contest, they cry, "Sufficient."

———

How this all works is mano a mano. Two guys line up opposite each other, try to grab each other's collars for purchase, and then kick at the foe's shins until either of them collapses to the ground, the equivalent of a technical knockout. Presumably, tubs of Neosporin and bandages are standing by.

These showdowns are conducted on a best 2-out-of-3 basis. There is a referee on the spot governing matters, perhaps if someone kicks too high or low. Points can be accumulated if neither hits the dirt.

It is an understatement to note that not only is kicking accuracy and power required, but the inner fortitude to withstand pain. In some general summaries of shin kicking, there are comments that at times some competitors wore steel-toed shoes. That could not have been a pretty picture. It is also a grisly thought to read that in the past, some shin kickers toughened up by banging hammers on their shins. The current rules specify only soft shoes can be worn. Regardless, it seems that more willpower is needed for shin kicking than kickball.

SEPAK TAKRAW

It's a virtual lock that only 1 in a million Americans have heard of this sport at all, and it's doubtful they can spell it or even pronounce it without doing research.

However, this is a big-deal sport in Malaysia and Thailand, even though not even ESPN in the old days at 3 a.m. would show the World Series of Sepak Takraw. Other Asian countries that embrace Sepak Takraw are Myanmyr, Vietnam, Laos, and the Philippines.

—

Okay, you've been in suspense long enough. The basic utensil of sepak takraw is a kickball, but not the kind of kickball elementary school kids play with in gym glass. That would be too easy. No, sepak takraw is pretty much volleyball with your feet. There is a net in 3-on-3 play, and much like the volleyball we all know and love, the players must keep the ball going back and forth over the net.

—

Look ma, no hands. That's because unlike volleyball, the players cannot employ their hands to keep directing the bouncing ball back and forth. Feet are key elements, but knees can also be used. The chest is okay, and the chin is legal. If you want to take a shot to the jaw and keep the ball going, it might be like being whacked with a piece of furniture. Certainly, in that part of the world, the game seems no weirder than soccer, where of course the ball can be propelled by a player's head.

—

Also unlike volleyball, where the ball is made of softer rubber and leather, the ball in sepak takraw is made of a harder material called rattan. One thing is certain: Players must be acrobatic to succeed in the sport.

—

Although it is probably not coming to Yankee Stadium anytime soon, there is a World Cup championship of sepak takraw. Believe it or not, even if there is no team nearby, a USA Takraw

Association was formed in 1996. Americans are fairly adept at the game, though they compete in Division II on the world scene.

HORNUSSEN

This is definitely not a sport on the tip of tongues in downtown Des Moines. Invented in Switzerland around 400 years ago, this is a sport where the main implement is a puck called a Nouss, as in a hockey puck. Knocked with a stick, the puck, which is made of wood, can zoom at up to 187 miles an hour, which is a reason players wear helmets.

Like baseball, 1 team bats at a time. Weaponry used to deflect the Nouss away is called a catch board. The flat board is mounted on a stick. One team of 18 competitors seeks to move the Nouss as far as possible down the field. (Perhaps this can be compared to moving a football?) The team tees off like golf, only from a ramp. The other team tries to keep it out of its zone. There is a neutral zone in the middle, but scores are recorded based on where the puck lands.

Games last 3 or 4 hours, and 4 quarters are played. Each player on a team must hit the Nouss twice. Hornussen has only about 8,000 players in its home base of Switzerland, but the game has bulged beyond the country's borders of late, and sure enough a small band of Americans has given it a try.

CAPOEIRA

From the country that gave you Carnivale, the epic bacchanal of parties, comes a sport that seems to promise casualties set to music. They actually call it the Dance of War, so that isn't too much of a reach.

—

Capoeira is a Brazilian martial art, but with the music you can draw blood and imitate a ballerina at the same time. It doesn't hurt to have a little bit of gymnastics ability, either. Some say the roots of capoeira date to the 16th century and it was invented by African slaves more consciously focusing on dance and religion than combat.

—

Whatever the case, capoeira was given a special exalted status by UNESCO as an "intangible cultural heritage." UNESCO stands for the United Nations Educational, Scientific and Cultural Organization and is based in Paris. Its task is to identify and promote international peace, law, human rights, and understanding through cultural reforms. Maybe UNESCO even understood capoeira.

> Still some sports fans in those countries may need translators to comprehend capoeira.

YUKIGASSEN

It's not clear if you can earn a varsity letter in Yukigassen or not, but even if the Japanese word is virtually unknown in the United States, the principles of the game sound a bit like those of dodgeball. The point is to cream your opponent with snowballs. The translation of Yukigassen is "snow battle."

Kids have done this for centuries in cold-weather American locations, but pretty much randomly, not in such organized fashion.

The charm of this sport is obvious: small-school war without deadly weapons. In daily life, it is considered bad form to throw things at other people. This suspends the rules. Clearly, a handy abundance of snow is a necessity, but surely it is cheaper to arm a village than go into Dick's Sporting Goods and buy six canoes or something.

Under the rules of the game, or the laws of the jungle, 2 teams of 7 players face off. Often, their weapons of mass destruction are rolled ahead of time. Unlike in comparatively innocent childhood snowball throwing, where nobody thought about the consequence of injury, some planning has gone into these showdowns. Helmets are worn, no doubt to protect against brain damage from Aroldis Chapman-like 100 mph fastballs.

This game originated on the Japanese island of Hokkaido, so naturally enough, Hokkaido is the host of an annual world championship. Snowball fighting did spread from the island to such nations as Canada, Norway, Sweden, and Russia, all places that get their fair share of snow. On American turf, Alaska has dabbled in the sport, and it would not be far-fetched to see an Alaska-Minnesota challenge.

UNICYCLE HOCKEY

For those who think that unicycling is confined to the circus, time to broaden your horizons, although one might ask if they like hockey so much, why don't they play it on ice? This is a very weird sport. Unicycle hockey? Including a unicycle as the method of transportation on the court is extremely peculiar in and of itself and would seem to disqualify many would-be players right off the bat.

This game is played while speeding back and forth up the court while carrying a hockey stick and trying to score goals in a net. Five players compete at once on a team, although there is no permanent goalie. If the opposing team mounts a rush and threatens to score a goal, players take turns defending the net, although usually 1 player stays back farther than his teammates as more or less the last line of defense.

A court is supposed to be 38 to 49 yards long and 21 to 27 yards wide. It should also have rounded, not squared, corners. In lieu of a puck, a tennis ball is used as the object to swat around.

> The main areas of the sport are focused in Australia, Germany, and Switzerland, where games are played under the watchful eyes of the governing body of the International Unicycle Federation. The teams in those nations are more developed, but unicycle hockey is a club sport in several other countries.

Unicycle hockey is insinuating itself into the United States with Minnesota apparently having the biggest club in the country, even if the state's heart truly lies with the real-deal, better-loved ice hockey. Someone there noted unicycle basketball was once tried but fizzled out.

BOG SNORKELING

Anyone who has ever visited Hawaii and done anything except lie around on a beach working on obtaining a sunburn has probably gone snorkeling in the pristine waters. Amazement at the beauty of the water and the marine life swimming past usually follows.

That is one reason it seems foolish to waste a snorkeling experience by racing across a bog. Yuck. This weird sport was invented in England, where it seems the word snorkeling is spelled with 2 *l*s. England? Come to think of it, the country must have too many inhabitants with too much time on their hands to dream up so many activities like this.

As spectators (yes, they have fans) watch, individuals, often attired in wet suits (not mandatory but advised), jump into a water-filled trench 60 yards long and propel themselves 2 lengths of a peat bog. Basically, the official gear is a snorkeling mask and flippers. It is illegal to swim with your arms. All forward motion must stem from flipper flapping.

As an encouragement to compete in this lunacy, one is invited to explore the definition of a peat bog. In part, it is said to be "a deposit of dead plant material." The words "mire" and "quagmire" also come up, so contestants can be assured the actual course will not be scenically inviting like Hawaiian waters. Perhaps a subdefinition of bog snorkeling could be "making something out of nothing."

The origin of bog snorkeling dates back to England in 1976. Astonishingly enough, some guys sitting around a bar were drinking when they came up with the idea. It was not mentioned how long they had been sitting around the bar drinking when they came up with the idea, but one might guess they were not on their first pint.

Anyone questioning whether bog snorkeling is considered a sport should be informed there has been a world championship contested since 1985. Winning times have declined (as in most other timed sports) over the years to where the world record is just under 1 minute, 20 seconds.

> **Not sure if every contestant must have shots afterward to prevent disease.**

ZORBING

Zorba the Greek did not invent zorbing. A zorb is an orb, where a person enters an inflatable plastic bubble and rolls down a hill as fast as possible. Once pushed off, gravity takes control in zorbing, and the inhabitant gets to shout, "No brakes!"

While that may be the most thrilling and chilling form of zorbing, this sport can also be played on level ground. That takes much more work for the driver to propel the orb around, although he may have a bit more say in where it is going.

A critical question about zorbing is "How does the zorber breathe when encased in the orb?" That would seem to become an even more important issue when the daring zorb on water. A person can stand up and walk inside the orb to send it forth.

> This is not a completely innocent sport. People have been known to die from collisions in orbs and lack of air.

While orbs of some sort have been around at least since 1973, *zorbing* became an official word in the Oxford English Dictionary only in 2001.

A London-based group with the self-explanatory name of the Dangerous Sports Club (the group was credited with creating modern bungee jumping) once built a giant zorb that was about 75 feet across and housed 2 chairs. Zorbing in style.

OSTRICH RACING

Unlike for thoroughbred horse racing with its signature Kentucky Derby, Americans would be hard-pressed to name a single well-known ostrich race. There are very few places in the US where you can see barns housing ostriches, or ostriches going through their morning race pacing.

———

Ostrich racing got its start in Africa, but it has been performed in Florida for quite some time. Ostrich farms going back to 1890 led to ostrich race tracks and the offering of tourist rides for 50 cents. Just as in thoroughbred racing, jockeys rode the animals, and they were encouraged to weigh less than 150 pounds if they wanted to get anywhere. The ostrich, being smaller than the horse, had an intolerance level for too much weight but when let loose could attain sprinting speeds of nearly 45 mph. Ostriches have huge strides. No jogging for the ostrich, but stride lengths of 16 feet. Hang on to your hat! Since ostriches have also been known to buck their riders, they may have something in common with saddle bronc riding in rodeo, too.

———

Flash-forward more than a century, and you can still make travel plans for the Great American Ostrich Races in the Chandler Ostrich Festival in Arizona.

CHAPTER 2
WEIRD SPORTS INJURIES

TURK EDWARDS

Turk Edwards was a first-class lineman in the National Football League during the league's leather-helmet days, starting his career in 1932. Inducted into the Pro Football Hall of Fame in Canton, Ohio, in 1969, he had a solid coaching career between his pro retirement and his enshrinement.

After starring in college at Washington State University, the 6-foot-2, 265-pound Edwards was a coveted pro prospect.

It is the peculiarity of Edwards's injury-caused retirement that invokes the weird. Representing his Washington Redskins in the coin toss in a 1940 game against the New York Giants, Edwards participated in the routine event, shook hands with New York captain Mel Hein, turned to jog back to his team bench—and tore up a knee.

As Edwards made his move away from midfield, one of his cleats got caught in the grass. A knee that was previously often injured became twisted and then popped out of place. The simple maneuver, done before every single game by every single captain, ended his professional career.

What a way to remember your last game. Now that's weird. It gives new meaning to the words "fluke injury." Edwards's injury might be the most bizarre in the history of the NFL, certainly to such a prominent player doing the least to deserve it.

JIMMIE JOHNSON

The 7-time NASCAR champion is 1 of the greatest stock-car racers of all time. When one thinks about injuries to these death-defying drivers, they usually pop up in the realm of an automobile crash during a race while traveling about 200 mph.

While scary, that is the noble way for a race-car driver to suffer an injury. Which is probably why the original explanations for a Johnson injury incurred in a motorized vehicle were a bit sketchy and of the cover-your-tracks variety.

In 2006, Johnson was attending a celebrity golf tournament when it was reported he had fallen out of a golf cart (top speed probably 20 mph) and broke his left wrist. That was embarrassing enough, but it turned out there was more.

Johnson wasn't exactly riding inside the golf cart during the event when his mishap occurred. He was actually, as it later came out, "horsing around." That was the explanation for how he came to be lying on top of said golf cart. Presumably, not wearing a seat belt.

Apparently, when Johnson was busy playing around, his golf partner at the wheel hit a berm, and the impact threw Johnson off the cart. Oops. Johnson has fared much better around vehicles when he was the driver.

> Since it was December, the regular 2006 season had ended. It was announced Johnson would need 4 weeks to recuperate, making him ready to participate in the Daytona 500 2007 opener in February.

PAULO DIOGO

Paulo Diogo really paid for a postgoal celebration. Diogo, from Switzerland, was so thrilled when his team scored a goal in a 2014 match, he ran over to a metal fence, climbed up, and yelled to fans. This was the kind of act Helio Castroneves indulged in when he won the Indianapolis 500 not 1 but 3 times. The fans adored it.

Mountain climbers often say they face the most dangers on the descent in the Himalayas or on other large peaks. Well, Diogo did not make it back to earth safely. He caught a finger on the fencing and left part of it there.

Proving his true love to his wife, he had been wearing his wedding band during the game action, and the wedding band catching on the metal caused the mishap. Stunned, Diogo began searching for the missing portion of his finger as the remnant gushed blood. It was not a pretty picture. In fact, it was a somewhat nausea-provoking picture, and media outlets slapped warnings to the squeamish watching their coverage.

In the ultimate case of adding insult to injury, the referee, clearly a coldhearted fellow, penalized Diogo for taking too long in his celebration, although what was really taking so long was prospecting for the missing portion of his digit.

Once recovered, Diogo packaged up the missing piece of his finger, rushed to the hospital, and underwent surgery. Only the finger could not be reattached.

After that, Diogo probably left his wedding ring at home on game days.

BRIAN ANDERSON

Irons are hot, right? Everyone knows that. Yes, it takes time for them to warm up after you get them going, but the heat is a key element in smoothing out that pesky wrinkle in the dress pants or a shirt that has been stuffed inside a suitcase too long.

Usually, the biggest risk people take with irons is quickly pressing a finger against the surface to test the temperature. That should tell you what's up. So, what was going through Brian Anderson's head in 2001 when he chose to test the temperature of his iron by rubbing it against his face? This was right before Anderson was scheduled to pitch the 3rd game of the World Series for the Arizona Diamondbacks against the New York Yankees.

> You guessed it, the iron was hot. It was hot enough to sear his cheek or, as someone else put it, *fry* his cheek. The results were not pretty.

It was kind of tough to duck the attention under the glare of the World Series spotlight, but Anderson did not try to do so. "I was getting ready to iron a shirt," he said. "You know, on the road, some irons you plug in and have to turn on. Some you plug in and they're automatically on? There've been so many that I plugged in, would wait 5 minutes, go to use it, and it wouldn't be the 1 you flip on . . . I picked up the iron, held it to my face to feel the heat, and was trying to look around the corner [of it] to watch the game. I just put my cheek right on it. It didn't take much, and it fried the side of my face. What are you going to do?"

> One piece of advice would be to let the wrinkles stand.

Although Anderson did not suffer an injury in another odd episode, he was also a guy who once rose from bed at night naked and sleepwalked into the corridor of his hotel. As a matter of fact, no, he didn't happen to have his key with him on that occasion. No pockets.

STEVE SPARKS

Former knuckleball right-hander Steve Sparks was toiling in the Milwaukee Brewers' minor league system when a mistake in judgment halted his progress to the majors. Sparks, who won 59 games during 9 seasons in the big leagues, incurred a serious shoulder injury.

One day, he attempted to tear a phone book in half. However, the phone book tore cartilage. The injury cost him enough time on the disabled list that he was not brought to the Show for a year.

"I had it halfway ripped apart when my shoulder popped out," Sparks recalled. "The lists are going to come out with the weirdest sports injuries of all time. I'm always high up on the list."

> And here he is. He forgot Superman, not Clark Kent, could tear the phone book in half.

KEVIN MITCHELL

A member of the 1986 World Series champion New York Mets, a 2-time All-Star, and the 1989 National League Most Valuable Player, Kevin Mitchell experienced several highs during his career. but the weirdest thing that probably ever happened to Mitchell was being injured by a doughnut. One day, he softened up a chocolate doughnut by warming it up in a microwave. However, when he bit into it, something was wrong because the chomp cracked a tooth. Grimacing in pain, Mitchell tossed the sweet treat in the garbage.

Mitchell had to undergo root canal surgery and was a few days late reporting to San Francisco Giants' spring training.

> # Maybe Mitchell forgot to put the timer on defrost.

ADAM EATON

Are baseball players too fragile compared to boxers or others in tough-guy sports? They play a noncontact game but seem to lead the world in self-inflicted wounds.

Pitcher Adam Eaton (not to be confused with outfielder Adam Eaton) played in the majors between 2000 and 2009 and was employed by the San Diego Padres when he did enough harm to himself to draw blood.

Attempting to open a very well-sealed DVD, he gave up on his bare hands and resorted to a pocket knife to extricate the disc from the package. It was a rational thought, but execution was lacking, and Eaton stabbed himself. His injury was not to a finger or palm as might be projected, but to his stomach. He only needed 2 stitches, but no doubt the ribbing he took from teammates was more painful.

As far as big-picture injuries go, the damage was minor. Eaton's next start was put back just 2 days. He did admit he had overlooked the childhood lesson of always cutting away from yourself with a sharp implement.

TOO MUCH PLUCKIN'

The phrase "practice makes perfect" is an hoary aphorism applied to many endeavors, especially across the sports world. Repetition is regarded as a path to success for hitters in the batter's box, pitchers on the mound, marathoners running miles, or basketball players shooting from outside the three-point line.

However, the flip side of practice making perfect could be the equally well-worn comment "too much of a good thing." That is probably when doctors coined the phrases "repetitive strain" or "carpal tunnel syndrome."

Joel Zumaya was a rookie pitcher for the Detroit Tigers in 2006 when the team advanced to the American League Championship Series. Suddenly, Zumaya came down with an unexplained case of wrist inflammation and was not available from the bullpen. It wasn't until sometime later that general manager Dave Dombrowski revealed that Zumaya's problem originated with too much activity on the PlayStation 2 game "Guitar Hero." For the time being,

Zumaya was prevented from becoming a pitching hero because of his desire to be a guitar hero.

> Shades of Zumaya. Early in the 2018 season, Boston Red Sox star hurler David Price missed a start due to injury. Although Price denied it, team officials suggested the reason why Price had to rest his left hand was that he spent too much time playing video games.

In contrast to these pitchers who may have overdone it, a 2017 study suggested kids may benefit from avid video-game playing in 2 ways. They may attain hand-eye coordination and development more quickly and be taught to think fast, all traits leading to athletic success.

WHEN GOOD INTENTIONS GO BAD

Those who enjoy slapstick humor probably chuckle when a baseball teammate sneaks up behind a player who may have bashed the game-winning hit just before he is about to be interviewed by a television reporter and has a shaving cream pie squashed into his face.

We have seen it so often in recent years, it has almost become a cliché that such an incident will break out to decorate the hero-of-the-moment's face. Observers scream with delight and laugh their heads off. It is part of the boys-will-be-boys characteristic attributed to young men who play a game for a living.

There was, however, an exception to this pattern. Chris Coghlan was the reigning National League Rookie of the Year for the Miami Marlins during the 2010 season when teammate Wes Helms clouted a walk-off single to win a game. Afterward, Coghlan ran up to Helms brandishing a shaving cream pie, took a leap, and when he came down, Helms's dignity may have been violated, but Coghlan's knee was injured.

Coghlan went on the disabled list, underwent season-ending torn meniscus surgery, and faced a long rehabilitation. Coghlan probably never wanted to shave again, never mind pie anyone in celebration.

SNEEZING IS BAD FOR YOU

Most people get annoyed when they have sneezing fits at a rat-a-tat-tat, machine-gun pace, whether it is due to allergies or a cold. Others keep their distance, since they worry about catching something, even if the cause is simply hay fever. They shout, "God bless you," over their shoulders as they retreat.

———

Unless the sickness is a really bad cold morphing into the flu or something like that, the sneezing pattern may subside in a day or so. An allergy attack may last just minutes, although such attacks may return regularly over a period of weeks if atmospheric conditions are just wrong.

Sammy Sosa, mostly with the Chicago Cubs, was 1 of the most productive home-run hitters of all time with 609 4-baggers accumulated over an 18-year career. When you play that long, you expect to incur injuries now and then. Those aches and pains add up, and you sit out a couple of games to get well.

While preparing to play a game against the San Diego Padres during the 2004 season, Sosa erupted with 2 violent sneezes. As it was said at the time, this was nothing to sneeze at. Sosa actually sprained a ligament in his back and could not play. Indeed, Sosa so thoroughly injured himself, he had to sit out for a month.

In 2015, when Toronto Blue Jays outfielder Kevin Millar sneezed so hard that he strained an oblique muscle, the injury was instantly compared to Sosa's of 11 years earlier.

> "God bless them."

TRIFECTA OF DISASTER

Glenallen Hill was a lifetime .271 hitter for 7 teams in the major leagues between 1989 and 2001, including the Chicago Cubs twice. Although he never received much praise for his erratic fielding, Hill was a member of the 2000 New York Yankees World Series champions.

Yet for all his fine batting work on the field, Hill will be forever remembered as someone who was forced onto the disabled list for 1 of the most bizarre injuries in the history of the sport.

The story of how Hill injured himself belongs not only in the pantheon of weirdest sports injuries, but perhaps as a tale told by late-night TV characters such as Vampira.

This happened to be the summer of the release of the horror movie *Arachnophobia*, about a deadly spider stalking and killing people as John Goodman and Jeff Daniels try to save the world.

One night during the baseball season while Hill was playing for the Toronto Blue Jays, he innocently laid his head down for his nightly rest. Only he dreamed of dangerous, killer spiders in his nightmare. Bad enough. But in his desperate desire to elude them, Hill began sleepwalking, which turned into sleeprunning, never a good thing. Unbelievably, the situation turned worse yet. While he was in his unconscious state, dashing about his house in fear, Hill crashed over a glass table, shattering it. Hill cut his feet, knees, and elbows in many places, splashing blood around his house, and, still unaware while frantically fleeing the imaginary spiders, he fell down a flight of stairs, too.

By the time Hill woke up, with the help of his alarmed wife, he was a mess and in dire need of medical assistance. Hill even gave skeptical newsmen a tour of his still-bloodsplattered home to buttress the reality of the story. Hill spent 20 days on the disabled list. Teammates with no mercy promptly dubbed Hill "Spiderman."

Although granting the admission that he was scared of spiders, Hill said the circumstances were a fluke. After his playing days ended, Hill went into coaching and minor-league managing. In 2017, while in charge of the Albuquerque Isotopes, he demonstrated his heralded fear of spiders was in the past. He posed for photographs while a king-sized tarantula casually made its way across his bare arm.

HE DIDN'T SEE IT COMING

Cleveland Browns offensive tackle Orlando Brown received a far more serious penalty than anticipated in a 1999 game when he jumped offside. Normally a routine 5-yard penalty for the infraction, Brown's career was essentially ruined by a strange sidebar to the play: the tip of the penalty flag blinded him in his right eye.

As Brown, whose nickname was "Zeus," made his false-start move, official Jeff Triplette blew his whistle and threw a penalty flag. Somehow, the yellow bag, which was weighted down with ball bearings (much heavier than a kerchief-like object), sailed through the air, traveled through a space in Brown's face mask, and hit him in the right eye. This was nearly impossible to accomplish given the limited amount of space in the mask.

Brown was taken out of the game. Although Triplette immediately apologized, Brown became enraged over his problem and raced back onto the field to push him to the ground. Brown was then ejected and suspended, although the suspension was reduced when the extent of his injury became known.

Likely, the referee's throw could not have been duplicated with such accuracy more than once in 10 tries at best. However, this fluke toss created serious damage. Brown underwent treatment for years. He was declared legally blind in the eye and spent 3 years rehabbing the injury before he could again see well enough to suit up, this time for the Baltimore Ravens. Brown sued the NFL and was awarded $15 million in a settlement.

> **Brown was 40 years old when he died from complications related to diabetes.**

IT WASN'T INDIGESTION

Los Angeles Kings hockey player Dustin Penner really liked his wife's cooking. Although he was trying to watch his weight and stay in shape during the 2011–12 season, he was not going to deprive himself of her homemade pancakes for breakfast.

He leaned over to "dip into some delicious pancakes my wife made," Penner explained, noting there was no dramatic movement or unusual activity going on, when with no warning his back completely seized up. Penner was almost paralyzed in his chair at the kitchen table, unable to rise without pain.

—

On that day, he said, his wife had to help him get dressed. Penner eased himself into his car and managed to drive to the team's home rink, where he underwent treatment.

—

It is not known if this is the only case of a professional athlete being sidelined due to an injury incurred while eating breakfast food, but this was definitely the most highly publicized such case.

KENDRYS MORALES: DO NOT PARTY ON

Happy to sad in the time it took to circle the bases. Los Angeles Angels hitter Kendrys Morales blasted a game-winning, grand-slam home run in a 5–1 victory over the Seattle Mariners in 2010. His teammates went crazy, storming out of the dugout and waiting at home plate to greet him.

> Enthusiastic about the bomb and the reception, as Morales approached home plate, he leapt in the air, an emphatic gesture of stepping on home.

As Morales scored the run, teammates were poised to hug him, tackle him, and mob him in celebration. As they feted their hero of the night, Morales ended up lying on the ground, a bone in his leg already damaged from his ill-timed landing on the plate. What was initially announced as a broken left leg was later reported as a broken ankle with a torn ligament, to boot. And a boot was pretty much what Morales needed for recuperation.

Everyone was stunned, but in the moment, nobody had any idea how serious the injury was. In a startling development, Morales went on the disabled list, required 2 surgeries, and did not play another game until the 2012 season, 23 months later. The extent of the ankle damage was significant. Morales needed 6 screws and a pin implanted.

Man, what a bummer.

> Although he healed and was able to return to the majors, Morales lost a big chunk of prime playing time to this fluke injury.

JOBA CHAMBERLAIN TIMES 2

For a period of time after Joba Chamberlain joined the New York Yankees in 2007, he became the talk of the town as a relief pitcher, and he played for the club during its 2009 World Series run.

———

Unaware of what the future held in the weirdness sweepstakes, in October of 2007, the right-handed thrower found himself in the midst of an awkward and bizarre situation. Throwing in the second game of the American League Division Series against the Cleveland Indians, Chamberlain was caught up in what could have been a mini-horror movie.

———

Abruptly, out of nowhere, Chamberlain and other players on the diamond at Progressive Field were besieged by swarms of tiny insects. It was an invasion of massive numbers of midges, which might have been okay if the guys were involved in fly fishing, not trying to advance in the American League playoffs. This became known as the "Bug Game."

———

As time was called, Yankee clubhouse officials raced to the mound to drench Chamberlain in insect repellent. It was the equivalent of being hosed down. However, nothing deterred the bugs. A correlation might be made between the annoying insects and what happened on the field, but there was no successful remedy for either development. Chamberlain threw 2 wild pitches, and the Indians scored and ended up winning the game, 2–1, and the series.

> Mostly, Chamberlain had his pride hurt in this debacle rather than receive any major physical injury. That would come later.

It is possible Chamberlain stands out as the leading single Major League player at the center of 2 astoundingly weird incidents. There is no Elias Sports Bureau category for this, but his experiences are hard to top. Besides the insects, Chamberlain was felled by injury in a particularly odd manner.

In 2012, prior to the start of the season, Chamberlain was playing with his son, Karter, on trampolines in Tampa. They were jumping back and forth between them, and the elder Chamberlain took a fall and suffered a compound fracture of his ankle. Some people on the scene suggested Chamberlain lost so much blood from the accident that he was in danger of bleeding out and dying before being taken elsewhere for treatment. The first news stories about the trampoline accident indicated that.

———

However, when Chamberlain met with sportswriters 5 days later, he denied that the injury was that gory.

———

Chamberlain, like many other players, accumulated baseball injuries during his career, but he is certainly the only 1 who was bugged on the mound by insects and also had to go on the disabled list for being attacked by a trampoline.

CAL RIPKEN JR: HE FORGOT TO DUCK

Hall of Fame shortstop Cal Ripken Jr. of the Baltimore Orioles gained the most notoriety from his lengthy and outstanding career by becoming Major League Baseball's ultimate Iron Man by playing in a record 2,632 straight games.

———

Ripken broke Lou Gehrig's 56-year-old record of appearing in 2,130 straight games, and he did so by playing though many nagging injuries. It was an epic achievement. After he topped Gehrig's record, but before he terminated his own streak, Ripken suffered 1 of the strangest injuries of all time. He was just fortunate it happened in an exhibition game, though a high-profile one.

———

As of the July 9, 1996, All-Star game, Ripken's record stood at 2,238 consecutive games played. As if to offer proof that only a fluke incident stood between a consecutive games record holder and a much shorter record, Ripken broke his nose while the American League team picture was being taken.

Just after the traditional squad photo was snapped, the platform the players stood on began to give away. It tilted, and Roberto Hernandez, a relief pitcher with the Chicago White Sox, sought to maintain his balance. He threw his hands up, and his arm shot out. His elbow struck Ripken in the nose, breaking it and causing bloodshed.

> Hernandez was horrified, believing this little accident might cause the end of Ripken's playing streak.

"I thought I'd have to get a damn bodyguard the next time we went to Baltimore," Hernandez said. "I knew that if it ended the streak, I'd be dead."

Ripken could have scratched himself from the All-Star game, but he did not. He went into the clubhouse, looked in the mirror, and said, "Yuck." A trainer popped the nose back into place, and he went onto the field. Ripken went 0-for-3 at the plate in the AL's 6–0 loss to the National League.

———

When Ripken asked if he was worried he would be unable to assume his regular place in the lineup when the Orioles resumed the regular season 2 days later, Ripken professed himself to be a swift healer and was sure he would be able to appear. Naturally, he did so, continuing his playing streak.

———

Indeed, Ripken's main reaction was that he was embarrassed to suffer an injury during the taking of a darned team photograph.

RANDY ORTON: TERRIFIC RECUPERATIVE POWERS

Although professional wrestling was long derided as fake by many observers, and eventually the admission came that many matches were scripted with preordained results, the only thing nobody could deny was how much of a beating that wrestlers took. They were fortunate to hold their bodies together, even when some blows absorbed were staged like movie scenes.

———

These guys took a genuine hurting and needed doctors' help more regularly than most would admit. Randy Orton, 38 in 2018, was born in Knoxville, Tennessee, into a family of wrestlers who had distinguished careers. A third-generation grappler, Orton is 6-foot-5 and 250 pounds. He became the World Wrestling Entertainment's youngest champion at 24 in 2004.

> Orton, who says he has double-jointed shoulders, has still had numerous problems with those body parts. The highlight, or lowlight, of sorting out such damage occurred in 2015, when Orton reported a new shoulder injury, although not received in the ring.

His latest dislocation occurred at home while he was taking out the garbage. Supposedly, being as experienced with such issues as Mel Gibson in the *Lethal Weapon* movies, he promptly popped the shoulder back into place. Unlike the film scenes where Gibson, as Martin Riggs, simply bangs his shoulder against a hard surface and groans, it may have taken 3 hours to pop Orton's shoulder back where it belonged.

A quick fix it was not.

MOISES ALOU MISSTEP

Obviously, outfielder Moses Alou had good intentions. He was working out, not carousing in the middle of the night. He was trying to stay in shape, not drown in inappropriate liquid refreshment.

Yet none of that did him any good. At a time when the outfielder was a key power hitter for the Houston Astros and coming off a season in his early 30s when he slugged 38 home runs and drove in 124 runs, Alou hurt himself in the off-season while home in the Dominican Republic.

He fell off a treadmill and tore an anterior cruciate ligament in his knee. The injury was so bad that Alou had to miss the entire 1999 season. They always say accidents occur in the home.

While not explained, Alou must have hit the higher speed button at the wrong time, just as some huge denouement was breaking during a soap opera on the television set. After going to a doctor, Alou at first thought he was looking at a month's worth of rehab at worst. Then came the MRI diagnosis.

It never was stated what the mph level was on the treadmill when Alou took his tumble. It was just crazy that it happened.

ROGER CRAIG'S LADIES UNDERWEAR CUT

Right-handed pitcher Roger Craig was generally felt to have better stuff than his lifetime Major League record of 74–98 indicated. The main reason Craig's career mark was so far under .500 was due to being stuck with the New York Mets during their first 2 seasons of existence, when they were the worst team in baseball.

In consecutive years, Craig's record was 10–24 and 5–22. Craig also managed the San Diego Padres for a couple of years when that club wasn't very good, either. But he did have some very good seasons at the helm of the San Francisco Giants.

Craig's weird injury may come under the heading of "A gentleman never tells." He suffered a pretty good gash on his hand from a lady's bra strap. Craig kept quiet on the who, the how, and the why, but he did have a large bandage covering the wound. It seemed more like a teenage boy type of injury while being a klutz in the backseat of a car, but since Craig was well into adulthood, he never spoke of the details.

The players weren't sure how to clarify Craig's date success, but perhaps they said he got to second base.

GLENN HEALY PLAYED THE WRONG TUNE

The National Hockey League goaltender Glenn Healy was employed by the Toronto Maple Leafs in 2000 when he suffered a weird injury in the off-season. Somehow, he slashed his left thumb so badly that he needed 10 stitches to repair the gushing-blood cut.

> At the time, Healy was trying to repair his antique set of bagpipes.

Healy had a 15-year NHL career after coming out of Western Michigan University. One of his hobbies was playing the bagpipes. The timing of the injury was good for Healy, who was healed up by the time the next season began.

Ordinarily, Healy only played the bagpipes, he didn't wrestle them. Some have proclaimed Healy the best bagpipe player in NHL history, though it is unclear what the competition is.

JEAN PIERRE-PAUL BLEW UP FIREWORKS IN HIS HAND

In the summer of 2015, Jean Pierre-Paul was a star defensive end for the New York Giants in the National Football League. On July 4, Pierre-Paul, the son of Haitian immigrants, was home in Deerfield Beach, Florida, for the holiday.

Seized by a patriotic spirit for his adopted country, and more financially well-off than others in the neighborhood, Pierre-Paul invested $1,100 in fireworks to provide a treat on Independence Day. Like many others, despite being constantly warned by authorities, Pierre-Paul was injured in a fireworks accident.

Pierre-Paul received considerable bang for his buck, hauling the fireworks to the liftoff site in a U-Haul trailer. The football player was ready to call it a day before midnight, only a friend suggested they light off the last remaining handful of fireworks to clear out the vehicle.

Pierre-Paul was game and sought to set off the last of the bunch using a lighter. However, the wind picked up and kept blowing out the ignition of flame. When the firework stick went off with a loud explosion and a bright light, Pierre-Paul fell to the ground amid considerable smoke.

———

When that moment passed, Pierre-Paul realized he had a serious problem. His right hand was bleeding profusely and had incurred significant damage. Pierre-Paul quickly made a makeshift bandage, wrapping his shirt around his hand, then a friend rushed him to the hospital while he agonizingly looked at a hand that with skin gone vividly revealed ligaments and tendons.

———

After initial treatment, Pierre-Paul's right index finger was amputated. He then had a lengthy rehabilitation, and when he returned to the football field, he had to play wearing a large bandage. After a surgery, Pierre-Paul was able to play with a special glove instead of the padded covering.

JOSE CANSECO SHOOTS HIS HAND

During a 17-year Major League career, outfielder Jose Canseco bashed 462 home runs, won a Most Valuable Player award, and knocked in 1,407 runs. In 1 game in 1993 while playing for the Texas Rangers, he suffered a brutal injury—to his pride. A misjudged fly ball off the bat of Carmelo Martinez of the Cleveland

Indians bounced off Canseco's head and bounced over a fence for a home run.

———

As far as baseball history goes, some people felt Canseco shot himself in the foot by writing a book that in a controversial manner alleged performance-enhancing drug use by teammates, revelations that led to MLB investigations. However, Canseco subsequently did shoot himself in the left hand, initially blowing off a finger. In 2014, Canseco was cleaning a gun inside his Las Vegas home. He did not realize a bullet was in the chamber, and the gun went off. It took out a finger, but doctors were able to surgically reattach it.

A month or so later, Canseco announced the finger fell off during a poker game and he was going to sell it online, along with the gun. Soon after, he admitted he was joking about that and that his finger was hanging in there and not for sale.

TOO NEAT A FREAK

John Smoltz is a Hall of Fame pitcher whose hurling credentials are impeccable. He has also become a pretty solid broadcaster, too, but is haunted by 1 of the most bizarre injuries of all time.

—

There are 2 versions of the story, though it is generally known as the tale of how John Smoltz ironed himself. Not to be confused with the sport of Extreme Ironing, although perhaps this could qualify, Smoltz decided 1 day at the last minute that he did not want to leave the house with a wrinkled shirt on. However, the shirt was already on. What to do? (Did Smoltz know Brian Anderson?)

—

Supposedly, Smoltz was in a hurry, and rather than peel off the shirt and change into another, or take off the shirt and place it on the ironing board, he ran the iron up and down the wrinkles on the shirt, burning himself thoroughly through the thin material.

—

Allegedly, this incident occurred in 1990 and is often talked about. He was quoted in the *Atlanta Constitution* as saying, "I couldn't believe it. I've done it 5 or 6 times and never had that happen."

—

Smoltz began denying the veracity of the incident when it popped up again and again over the years.

"That is the most false thing I've ever heard," Smoltz said. "That got created 6 years ago, and it never left me. Ironing my shirt while it was on—that's the most absurd thing. It was made up. But it got on Arsenio Hall, CNN, everywhere. And what do you do to stop it?"

> At the least, he should have received an endorsement contract from a company that made a permanent-press shirt. The theme could have been "I know how important it is to dress without wrinkles."

FORGOT HIS KEYS

Taylor Heinicke was a backup quarterback for the Minnesota Vikings when he suffered an injury during the summer of 2016 leading up to training camp.

This was a self-inflicted error. Heinicke, who was living outside of Atlanta, came home 1 day and realized he was locked out of his house. Rather than call a locksmith, he decided he should be able to figure out a way to get in without outside assistance.

Heinicke said he came home after a late-night movie and nobody else was in the house, so he and a friend sought to break their way in through a double door. This breaking and entering did not go as planned. Heinicke said his foot slipped, broke through glass, and he slashed his ankle, obtaining a darned notable cut.

The cut was bad enough that he needed surgery. When Heinicke arrived for training camp, he was wearing a cast on his foot and admitted to being embarrassed by the klutzy incident. He said the movie he saw was *The Conjuring 2*. He liked it, but the cost was higher than expected.

DELAYED IMPACT

Colorado Rockies outfielder Carlos Gonzales was in the starting lineup as usual for a game in April of 2014 with nobody suspecting anything wrong with him. And there wasn't, initially. However, he had to leave the contest in the 6th inning, immediately raising speculation that he was suffering from some severe, unexplained injury.

It was definitely an unusual occurrence, but it did come with an explanation. The initial reason given for Gonzalez's departure was dehydration and dizziness. Was he sick with the flu or something? Nah. There was more to the story. Gonzalez hit the ground hard making a play during the game and swallowed his chewing tobacco. Gross.

Mostly, Americans hear about the evils of tobacco in the context that smoking causes lung cancer and chewing tobacco can cause lip cancer. This was a sneak attack from Gonzalez's tobacco. Everyone realizes chewing tobacco is meant to be chewed, not swallowed.

> Gonzalez apparently proved that argument. Chewing gum might not be designed for swallowing either, but if that substance had gone down his throat, it may not have churned his stomach quite as much.

DON'T GET TOO HAPPY

Bill Gramatica was a National Football League placekicker out of the University of South Florida who once booted a field goal 63 yards. That was worth celebrating. However, on another occasion, the Argentinian-born Gramatica celebrated too hard.

A 4th-round draft pick of the Arizona Cardinals in 2001, Gramatica won the job and was still in his rookie season during a December game against the New York Giants. Gramatica's strong leg produced a 42-yard field goal for 3 points, and he jumped up and down in celebration, only when Gramatica came down he tore an anterior cruciate ligament that required knee surgery. While helpful, the field goal did not lead to victory in that game either, and the ripple effect sent him to the sidelines for quite some time.

MEANT TO BE INGESTED, NOT SPREAD

Some like it hot, and Bret Barberie seemed to be 1 of those souls. When he downed a superhot chili pepper as part of a meal before the second baseman's Miami Marlins were scheduled to take the field for a game in 1994, he didn't think much of it.

Surely, a fan would at this point guess that the pepper was so hot it burned Barberie's mouth, or gave him indigestion. Not true. Instead, some remnant of the hot chili juice from the pepper apparently got on Barberie's fingers and was not all dried off.

When Barberie went to put in his contact lenses prior to the baseball game, he rubbed some of the residue into his eyes. Boy, that stung. He had to be scratched from the lineup that day because his vision was blurry.

> Assuming Barberie was not giving up pepper, next time he was probably going to be armed with a stash of wet wipes.

WILD ANIMALS ARE NOT PETS

Nolan Ryan, one of the greatest pitchers of all time with 7 no-hitters on his résumé and owner of 324 Major League victories, was a no-brainer Hall of Famer. He also made the no-brainer weird sports Hall of Fame because of a careless mistake in 1985.

At the time, Ryan was toiling for the Houston Astros while also maintaining a Texas ranch. One day, Ryan was driving around his property and stumbled upon 2 coyote pups that apparently had no mother in the vicinity. Assuming they would not fare well on their own, he gathered them up and toted them home.

Proving once again that no good deed goes unpunished, Ryan was subsequently bitten by 1 of the baby coyotes and had to visit the doctor. He had to undergo tests for rabies (the shots are notoriously painful), and he missed a turn in the pitching rotation. On top of that, the coyotes were confiscated because they were not considered to be suitable for home use.

CHAPTER 3
WEIRD SPORTS EVENTS

UNANTICIPATED WEIRDNESS: MIKE KEKICH AND FRITZ PETERSON

Sports trades happen all the time. Major League Baseball, National Football League, National Basketball Association, and National Hockey League teams spice up off-seasons and midseasons with player trades. Their goal is to immediately win a pennant or make the playoffs, or simply to get better and see where that takes them.

———

Fans are used to that, even if they are not always happy to lose a favorite player in exchange for someone who doesn't cut it. Franchises and clubs have long memories and recall which trades were the best ever and the worst ever.

———

However, this was an *ex officio* trade without team executives involved. What seemed like a good idea at the time to an inner core of folks was viewed bizarrely at the time though somehow has mostly been forgotten since, at least by those not born at the time.

———

Kekich and Peterson, both pitchers for the New York Yankees during the 1970s, were close friends, and so were their wives. They regularly socialized away from the ballpark. While the phrase *wife swapping* was in the lexicon, a description of couples swapping partners, it was usually seen as a temporary sexual liaison. This was different. On March 4, 1973, Kekich and Peterson announced they had not only traded wives, they traded families.

———

This did ignite a spree of discussion and controversy. While this was mostly the business of those involved, others were appalled, astonished, or merely curious. Alas, things did not work out as planned. While Peterson and his new wife embarked happily on a new course over the decades, Kekich and his new partner broke up without marrying. They chose for the kids to remain with their mothers.

———

All of this fueled gossip columns in a city where gossip is currency. Forty years later, Peterson called the choice "a love story," and he was only saddened because things did not work out for Kekich and his own ex-wife.

Kekich was gone from the Yankees
within months; Peterson stayed
around 1 more season.

RANDY JOHNSON'S WILDEST PUTOUT

Hall of Fame southpaw Randy Johnson was a feared pitcher during his career. Initially, hitters quaked in the batter's box because his fastball was so fast and his accuracy came under the heading of wild. Eventually, as Johnson tamed his stuff and embarked on his path of winning 303 big-league games, they shivered only because they couldn't catch up to his 98 mph tosses.

During a 2001 spring training game, the world got to see what could happen if a Johnson fastball collided with something more fragile than a baseball bat. Johnson, who was then playing for the Arizona Diamondbacks, reared back and hurled a pitch designed to fool San Francisco Giants hitter Calvin Murray.

The ball never reached the plate. A dove that had lost its way cutting through the ballpark lost its life in an instant when the ball struck it in midair. The unlikely confluence of ball and bird resulted in an explosion of feathers, with the bird virtually evaporating.

—

Murray, who was paid to keep his eye on the ball, delivered an eyewitness account: "It exploded, feathers and everything, just *poof!*" he said. "There was nothing but feathers laying on home plate. I never saw the ball, nothing but feathers."

> "Giants infielder Jeff Kent picked up the remains, but a groundskeeper was called upon to sweep up feathers."

Years later, Johnson, an accomplished photographer, started a photo business and used an upside-down, feathers-flying bird as part of the logo.

EDDIE GAEDAL'S MOMENT OF GLORY

The 1-at-bat wonder Eddie Gaedal may be the most famous player in Major League Baseball history whose lifetime average is .000.

On August 19, 1951, Gaedel was sent to bat by the St. Louis Browns in the 2nd game of a doubleheader against the Detroit Tigers as a publicity stunt. Gaedel, aged 26, stood 3-foot-7 and weighed 65 pounds. In the vernacular of the time, he was a midget, though that description has become an insult (for those who don't know).

Gaedel, who was recruited for this role by Browns owner Bill Veeck, wore a uniform with the number "$1/8$" on it. Gaedel was a member of the American Guild of Variety Artists. Veeck was renowned for dreaming up unusual events to entertain fans, and he was always searching for new gimmicks, especially if his teams were losing.

In those days, the Browns lost as much as anyone, so Veeck signed Gaedel to a contract in secrecy and sent it to the American League office over a weekend, ensuring it would not arrive before he employed his new player in a game.

It was the bottom of the first inning when Gaedel assumed his role pinch-hitting for Frank Saucier. When Gaedel walked to the plate, the umpire, Ed Hurley, summoned Browns manager Zack Taylor for a discussion. Although Taylor was only party to this plan because of his job, Veeck supplied him with a copy of Gaedel's signed contract for just such an eventuality.

Veeck told Gaedel not to swing at a pitch under any circumstances, and when it appeared Gaedel was waffling on that command, Veeck threatened to shoot him with a rifle from atop the stadium if he even hinted at doing so. Detroit catcher Bob Swift dropped to his knees to receive, and pitcher Bob Cain laughed as he threw 4 straight balls. Gaedel strolled to first base on his walk—stopping twice to bow to the crowd—and was removed for a pinch-runner. Baseball chastised Veeck for bringing someone so short to bat and he complained right back with a straight face, asking if New York Yankee shortstop Phil Rizzuto, who was 5-foot-6, shouldn't be classified as a dwarf.

> Gaedel still got his 15 minutes of fame. He died 10 years later at 36, but forever was enshrined in baseball lore.

TEETH TOO SHARP

Maybe it is because it seems I step removed from cannibalism, but outrage and horror follow when someone bites another human being. We are taught from a young age, just after teething, that it is inappropriate to bite your brother or sister.

———

Anytime someone in a public forum bites another person, rare as that is, the outcry is significant. Sometimes National Football League linemen allege that a member of the opposing team bit them when they were rolling around in a pileup at the line of scrimmage at the end of a play. Eyebrows are raised, but people just don't really know if they should believe the report.

———

That was not the situation when Mike Tyson and Evander Holyfield engaged in a boxing world heavyweight title match in 1997. This was the second time the protagonists met in the ring, and the theme of the night was "The Sound and the Fury." After the bout, the contest became known as "The Bite Fight."

———

About 8 months earlier, Holyfield had lifted Tyson's crown in a surprising result. This was a critical moment in Tyson's career. He could not afford another loss. The rematch was set for Las Vegas in late June. During a clinch in the second round, the men's heads collided. It was fairly apparent Holyfield head-butted Tyson, but referee Mills Lane ruled that the contact was accidental, not intentional. Tyson, who suffered a cut above his right eye, was angered by the call. A second meeting of the heads did not result in a meeting of the minds, either.

———

Tyson believed he was unfairly being taken advantage of, so in a sport where matters are basically taken into one's own hands, he took matters into his own bicuspids. In retaliation, Tyson chomped down on Holyfield's right ear. This was no minor thing. Tyson's intent was serious, and he nearly tore the ear off. Although he could have terminated the bout right there with a forfeit to Holyfield, when Lane stepped in, he instead deducted 2 points on scorecards from Tyson.

———

Tyson did not cease. When the action resumed, he bit Holyfield's left ear, though not as devastatingly. Lane stopped the fight, giving the win to Holyfield. The consequences were enormous for Tyson. He was fined $3 million, suspended from boxing for 15 months, and faced worldwide condemnation.

> In the long history of pugilistic encounters, nobody could recall an in-ring moment to compare.

DENNIS RODMAN I: LOOK AT ME

Never has such a National Basketball Association player's off-court behavior been so unique and offbeat. Dennis Rodman handled himself, sold himself, promoted himself, and attracted widespread gossip attention when he wasn't rebounding and helping to win championships for the Detroit Pistons and the Chicago Bulls.

———

As a player, the 6-foot-7, 210-pound forward was a rebounding machine, leading the league in that category 7 times. Unlike most of his peers, Rodman did not look to score first. He was an exemplary defender, more focused on stopping his assigned man from reaching the basket than bothering to reach the basket himself.

———

There is no question Rodman was an integral part of 5 championship victories for his 2 main allegiances during his 14-year career in the 1980s and the 1990s. After departing the NBA, Rodman continued playing basketball in smaller professional leagues and overseas.

———

The Pistons were called the Bad Boys at the height of their achievements, and Rodman was seen as the chief Bad Boy. However, his actual nickname was "Worm" because he got inside his opponents' heads.

Rodman was ahead of the cultural times in splashing tattoos all over his body, and he displayed so much metal in his nose, face, and ears that he could never pass an airport patdown without personal attention. His hair was died a bright blond. Rodman developed the habit of making outrageous statements, being linked to famous women like Carmen Electra and Madonna, throwing legendary parties, and publicly cross-dressing. Rodman crossed over to professional wrestling, teaming with Hulk Hogan, and appeared in some movies.

Rodman posed naked as part of the People for Ethical Treatment of Animals' "Rather Go Naked Than Wear Fur" campaign and was commissioner of the Lingerie Football League for a year. He hosted an MTV reality talk show, wrote more than 1 book about his life, and was twice a contestant on *Celebrity Apprentice*, with 1 of those appearances resulting in a $20,000 donation to the Make-A-Wish Foundation. He won $220,000 on the TV show *Celebrity Mole*, and it should also be noted that Rodman once entered the wife-carrying championships in Finland but had to withdraw because of ill-timed poor health.

In a fit of frustration, Rodman once kicked a cameraman who was innocently covering a game below the belt because he felt he was in the way. Another time, outraged at officials, Rodman ripped off his jersey during an argument and headbutted a referee. Even more seriously, Rodman had a highly publicized visit to a drug and alcohol rehabilitation clinic.

For all of that, Rodman's most clamorous nonbasketball appearances are times he shows up in public as a cross-dresser. Sometimes he has worn blond wigs, other times white wedding gowns and pink dresses. He once announced that he was bi-sexual—and was going to marry himself. Although Rodman did marry Electra at a 24-hour chapel in Las Vegas, that one might not even have played in Vegas.

> Basically, Rodman for years has made it clear he will do whatever he wants whenever he wants to do it.

DENNIS RODMAN II: BASKETBALL DIPLOMACY

Seeing as how Dennis Rodman had regularly splashed himself all over the pages of newspapers and magazines, and beyond their sports pages, it should not have surprised anyone when he became involved in world events. But it did.

Out of nowhere, Rodman began making regular visits to North Korea, 1 of the most closed and restrictive countries in the world and whose people have felt the sting of starvation and lived under the thumb of a series of family dictators for decades. In recent years, leader Kim Jong Un, the 3rd in the line of Communist leaders, regularly made threatening comments to the United States and South Korea, bellicose statements implying he could attack at any time. Although these were largely dismissed as propaganda, they began being taken more seriously around 2016, when Kim Jong Un flaunted various nuclear tests.

In 2013, Rodman brought basketball to North Korea and began bonding with the national leader. They were photographed together, and Rodman made several return trips. Because he was an unlikely diplomat, the world at large had no accurate reading if the man so often previously viewed as a cartoon character (an image he cultivated) was actually doing good work in the cause of peace. At 1 point, it did seem Kim Jong Un released a long-held American prisoner in the interests of friendship with Rodman.

At various times, Rodman brought other former players to North Korea for games and said he would train the North Korean basketball team. It seemed obvious that he had a rapport with the dictator. On one visit, Rodman brought a copy of President Donald Trump's book *The Art of the Deal* along as a gift.

When President Trump visited Singapore in the spring of 2018 for a summit conference with Kim Jong Un and the men shook hands and talked of mutual understanding and North Korea's possible willingness to eliminate its nuclear weapons stockpile inventory (although no action immediately occurred), there was a suggestion that Trump might be in line for the Nobel Peace Prize. By extension, that discussion made some wonder if Dennis Rodman, of all people, might be such a candidate, as well.

HE WAS OPEN

One of the most legendary gaffes in National Football League history occurred when Minnesota Vikings star defensive lineman Jim Marshall suffered a brief lapse in his concentration and ran the wrong way, to the opponent's end zone, during a game.

Marshall played in 282 NFL games and had his number 70 jersey retired by the Vikings, but many people remember him only for the biggest mistake of his career, not for all of his achievements.

Marshall played college ball at Ohio State and 1 year in the Canadian Football League before embarking on his long NFL career. On October 25, 1964, Minnesota was playing against the San Francisco 49ers. What began as a major defensive play ended up with Marshall being mortified about what he did. A 49ers player fumbled, and Marshall scooped up the loose ball. Thinking he was free and clear of being stopped, Marshall ran to daylight.

Only it was the wrong end zone. Marshall dashed 66 yards with the ball and then threw it down in celebration. Because he entered his own team's end zone, however, not the San Francisco end zone, the 49ers were awarded 2 points for a safety. Although the incident was personally embarrassing to Marshall, it was not that costly an error. Minnesota won the game anyway, 27–22.

In fact, usually overlooked is that Marshall played a major part in the game-winning play. Marshall sacked the 49ers' quarterback, causing another fumble. His defensive partner Carl Eller grabbed that ball and ran—the right way—for a touchdown.

The consequences of Marshall's mistake were minor, but the misplay lives on in NFL history and lore and is still viewed on old tapes, which helps perpetuate the periodic ridicule that comes Marshall's way.

There has been 1 other similar major ball-carrying mistake to rival Marshall's in the football world. And it predated his. In the 1929 Rose Bowl, a University of California player named Roy Riegels ran the wrong way with the ball. In a game against Georgia Tech, the first-team All-American and Cal captain was playing on defense and also picked up a fumble.

Riegels got spun around and instead of going straight ahead for the proper end zone 30 yards away, he ran in the other direction. After 69 yards, Riegels was tackled by a teammate who had been closing the gap between them and yelling for him to stop. Cal ended up on its own 1-yard line. The Bears promptly chose to punt to get out of trouble, but the kick was blocked and Tech got a safety out of the play, same as the 49ers' benefit decades later. In this instance, though, Tech won the game, 8–7.

> When Marshall ran the wrong way about 35 years later, Riegels sent him a letter reading, "Welcome to the club."

BUT HE GOT IT JUST RIGHT

Besides "Happy Birthday" and "The Star-Spangled Banner," 1 of the most frequently sung songs in the United States is "Take Me Out to the Ball Game."

While "The Star-Spangled Banner" became the National Anthem, "Take Me Out to the Ball Game" became baseball's anthem. Francis Scott Key was watching Americans defend Fort McHenry in the Battle of Baltimore during the War of 1812 when he penned his immortal words.

Jack Norworth was riding on a New York subway car when inspiration struck him and he jotted down his famous lyrics, later set to music by Albert Von Tilzer. The truly odd thing about Norworth's most memorable work is that he had never seen a baseball game in his life when he wrote the song in 1908.

Norworth wrote songs for a living, show tunes and the like, and outside the world of sport, his most famous tune and bestseller was "Shine On, Harvest Moon," cowritten with his wife, Norah Bayes. Baseball was popular enough in New York City during the 1st part of the 20th century, with the New York Giants, New York Highlanders, and the team that would become the Brooklyn Dodgers, so Norworth was not unaware. One day riding the subway, he saw an ad for Giants games at the Polo Grounds. Before he reached his stop a half-hour later, Norworth had his song written.

> "I was a professional songwriter," Norworth told a sportswriter years later. "I thought it was time for a baseball song and an idea struck me which I thought was pretty good."

Norworth did not attend a baseball game for 3 decades after he wrote the wildly popular song. Von Tilzer had also never seen a game before writing the music and did not attend one until 20 years after the song came out.

SLO' MO' HOOPS

Professional basketball did not become a staple of the American sports scene until right after World War II. Two leagues, the Basketball Association of America and the National Basketball League, vied for supremacy before merging in 1949.

Owners fretted low-scoring games would bore fans. There was no rule or motivation for teams leading to hurry play, so at times they held the ball for minutes, driving spectators crazy. One game in particular spurred action to introduce a 24-second shot clock.

On November 22, 1950, the Minneapolis Lakers and the Fort Wayne Pistons engaged in a contest regarded as perhaps the most boring and worst game of all time. The Pistons won, 19–18. Everyone agreed the game was a horror show for spectators and such cautiously played games like that would wreck the league, so Danny Biasone, owner of the Syracuse Nationals, lobbied his fellow club owners to approve a 24-second clock. Working with team general manager Leo Ferris, Biasone did the necessary research and could statistically demonstrate why 24 seconds was the proper length for each offensive possession.

The memory of that Pistons-Lakers game haunted league management. It was viewed as a stain the league had to eradicate. Only 3 *players* scored for the Lakers in that game, including superstar George Mikan, who somehow pumped in 15 points.

Stall ball remained part of college basketball for many years, but the NBA honchos regarded a repeat of such a game as a dreaded prospect. No more of that was the declaration.

TONYA AND NANCY

The figure skating assault orchestrated by the Tonya Harding camp to keep rival Nancy Kerrigan off the US Winter Olympic team for the winter games in Lillehammer, Norway, at the national figure skating championships in Detroit in early 1994 has been so publicized and been in the public eye for so long, sometimes it is forgotten just how bizarre the entire scenario was.

———

The lead-up to the US team selection included some of the most astonishing developments in sports history. Harding and Kerrigan were the 2 leading American candidates for the women's singles spots. They were extremely different people from different backgrounds.

In the elite world of figure skating, Harding was the outlier, poorer than the other top contestants, and it meant everything to her to make the American team. Kerrigan was more of a typical figure skating prospect.

On January 6th in Cobo Arena following a practice session, Kerrigan was attacked by a club-wielding assailant who bashed her on the leg. Shocked, battered, and bruised, Kerrigan withdrew from the competition. Harding won the national championship and a place on the Olympic team. Kerrigan was added to the team anyway. More than a month later, healed from the assault, Kerrigan won the silver medal. Harding did not place.

———

As pieces of the behind-the-scenes story filtered out, there was a tremendous backlash against Harding. It was revealed that Harding's ex-husband, Jeff Gillooly, and bodyguard Shawn Eckhardt hired a man named Shane Shant for the attack to better Harding's chances of making the Olympics. The 3 men eventually served time in prison for the plot.

———

Harding did not go to jail but pleaded guilty to efforts to hinder the prosecution against the trio of men and was sentenced to 3 years of probation, 500 hours of community service, and a $160,000 fine. In a separate investigation, the United States Figure Skating Association stripped Harding of the 1994 title and banned her for life from competing or coaching.

———

As the years passed, Kerrigan went on to live a private life in retirement. Periodically, in situations that seemed consistent with what may have been the weirdest sports scandal in history, Harding emerged in the public eye once more. A sex tape of her with Gilloolly appeared. She showed up at wrestling events and even tried professional boxing.

> A film called *I, Tonya* with serious chops painted a somewhat sympathetic portrait of Harding's difficult youth. The movie and its actors received critical acclaim and awards. In 2018, Harding competed on the TV show *Dancing with the Stars.*

CHUCK HUGHES: REST IN PEACE

A Detroit Lions wide receiver who played college football at the University of Texas at El Paso, Chuck Hughes is the only player to die on the field during a National Football League game.

Hughes was 28 years old and in his 2nd season with the Lions after playing his first 3 campaigns with the Philadelphia Eagles. Detroit was hosting the Chicago Bears on October 24, 1971, a game the Lions lost, 28–23, at Tiger Stadium in week 6 of the season. It was Hughes's 38th game as a pro, and he had 15 receptions in his career.

Hughes did not start the game but came in when someone was hurt. He nabbed a 32-yard pass from quarterback Greg Landry shortly before he collapsed on the field. After a play in which he did not figure, Hughes was running back to the Detroit huddle, just past the line of scrimmage. He keeled over, clutched his chest, and began convulsing.

> The closest player to Hughes was Chicago's legendary linebacker Dick Butkus, who realized Hughes was in distress and ran over to him. Butkus, a future Hall of Famer, signaled for assistance. Medical personnel converged on Hughes but could not save him.

An ambulance rushed Hughes to the hospital, but he was pronounced dead upon arrival. Teammates did not learn of Hughes's death until after the game. The cause of death was said to be a coronary thrombosis. An autopsy showed his arteries were 75 percent clogged, and it was noted his family had a history of heart disease.

In fact, Hughes had suffered a minor heart attack 7 weeks earlier but was not properly diagnosed. Hughes's wife said he had not been well in the days leading up to the game, and teammates said he was throwing up the night before the game. Hughes's wife later received a settlement from the hospital for not earlier diagnosing Hughes's heart problems.

Butkus was considered to be one of the most vicious hitters in football history, and he once said afterward that some fans blamed him for Hughes's death because he was captured on video standing near him. They believed he hit Hughes so hard he perished, but that was a distorted view of reality.

MANTI TE'O'S IMAGINARY FRIEND

In the fall of 2012, Manti Te'o was a star football player for Notre Dame, on his way to All-American recognition and a professional football career. If that wasn't enough, during the season, Te'o told sportswriters about his girlfriend, with whom he had connected a few years earlier and who had been tragically killed that fall in an automobile accident.

Te'o was an extraordinary college player who won several major college defensive awards his senior year, including those named for Chuck Bednarik, Bronko Nagurski, and Walter Camp. For 3 straight seasons, Te'o collected more than 100 tackles a year. It was suggested he might become the rare defensive player to win the Heisman Trophy (he finished second in the voting).

> Viewed as the type of good guy any daughter would be proud to bring home to her parents, Te'o was also a very religious person, grounded in his Mormon faith.

Supposedly, Te'o met Lennay Kekua after a Notre Dame–Stanford game in California in the fall of 2009. They remained in touch and became close. Reportedly, they rendezvoused in Hawaii a few times, Te'o's home state.

The plot thickened in 2012, when Te'o said his girlfriend had been in a terrible automobile accident in California. Then, when doctors were treating her, they learned she had leukemia. The couple talked on the phone nightly during these trying times, Te'o said.

In September, Te'o's grandmother passed away. Kekua sent a text of condolences to the family just as she was being released from the hospital herself. Within a day Te'o was contacted by Kekua's brother to inform him she also had passed away.

As the season progressed, so did Te'o. He became a national sensation as a player who was mourning his double personal losses. He spoke freely, if sadly, about his grandmother and girlfriend dying, simultaneously playing with renewed purpose.

Very slowly, very gradually, the entire story began unraveling. Te'o had never met Kekua but only had an online relationship with her. A woman with nothing to do with Te'o somehow figured out her likeness was being used, and she had suspicions about who had done it.

In the end, a former college football player was revealed to be behind this elaborate hoax that went viral. The gullible Te'o had

been a victim, hoodwinked on a national scale. He was also embarrassed on a national scale. Some people believed Te'o, motivated
by a desire for publicity, was in on the scam, though no such defin-
itive evidence materialized, and he stated the man behind the hoax
confessed to him in a telephone call.

> Te'o did go on to a pro career and
> currently plays for the
> New Orleans Saints.

UNIQUE PERFORMANCE-ENHANCING DRUG CHOICE

There have been other Major League baseball players through the
decades who were nicknamed Doc. But Dock Ellis was 1-of-a-kind
in more ways than expected. A right-handed pitcher who won 138
big-league games, Ellis once was photographed with a large number of curlers in his hair. That was a keeper.

Ellis is best-remembered for a claim he made some time after
pitching the finest game of his career. On June 12, 1970, in the
first game of a doubleheader, Ellis won, 2–0, over the San Diego
Padres. The masterpiece was a no-hitter, though only in the sense

that all no-hitters loosely come under that definition. After all, he did walk 8 men in that game. Nonetheless, the no-hitter label is impressive.

Fourteen years after the achievement, Ellis gave an interview with a peculiar account of his day. He said he actually believed the Pirates had an off-day in the schedule and while hanging out with his girlfriend opted to take a recreational drug to relax—LSD. It was only after his girlfriend was skimming the newspaper that he learned not only that the Pirates were scheduled to play, but he was down as the opening-game pitcher.

This set off a rather frantic scramble to the ballpark and a fascinating mound appearance. On the day he entered the record books for his no-hitter showing, Ellis said he threw the ball under the influence of LSD and didn't recall much about the event at all.

> "I can only remember bits and pieces of the game," Ellis said in 1984. "I was psyched. I had a feeling of euphoria."

Well, good for him. There have been other no-hitters, but never a pitcher who claimed that LSD made his day.

USC FOOTBALL PLAYER INJURED HOW?

In August of 2014, before the start of the college football season, a University of Southern California senior cornerback named Josh Shaw regretfully reported a double injury to the Trojans. According to Shaw, he incurred 2 ankle sprains when he jumped off the 2nd-story of an apartment building to rescue a 7-year-old nephew from drowning in a swimming pool.

He said he saw the boy struggling in the pool and that he did not know how to swim. That was quite the story, a bit of heroism a good explanation for dual ankle sprains. Only it wasn't true. A couple of days later, Shaw admitted he made the whole thing up—except for the ankle injuries.

Not everyone believed the original tale, so Shaw had to come clean. He was suspended from the team. It was not revealed at the time how he actually hurt both ankles, though a few months later, Shaw explained what really happened.

He said he and his girlfriend had an argument and she ran out of the apartment. He heard noise below and went out on the 3rd-story (not 2nd-story) apartment balcony and saw her talking to the police. His mind reeled, and he thought she was going to make up a story about him hitting her or something and get him arrested, so he did jump off the balcony trying to disappear for a little while. He knew the instant he hit the ground he had done some damage and was in so much pain he had to crawl away. That's when he made up the nephew story, because it sounded better than the reality.

> Shaw played the last 3 games of his senior season after recovering from the injuries and having his suspension curtailed. Since then, he has played for the Cincinnati Bengals in the NFL.

YOU GOTTA HAVE HEART

Practically every coach in every sport urges their players to dig deep and show they have heart when the going gets tough. But that is metaphorical. No coach ever imagined the lengths to which mixed martial arts combatant Jarrod Wyatt would take the message.

Wyatt, 29, from Crescent City, California, was a middleweight who won a couple of bouts but wasn't very well known in the sport until he crossed the Dracula line. On March 21, 2010, police responded to a phone call from Wyatt's then-home. When they arrived, they were stunned by the scene greeting them.

Taylor Powell, 21, Wyatt's friend and sparring partner, was dead. Wyatt was naked, with blood smeared all over his body. He promptly informed the police that he had killed Powell, cut out his heart and tongue, and roasted his heart in a wood-burning stove.

In the bizarre situation, it was concluded that after both men took hallucinogenic mushrooms, they completely lost touch with reality, convincing themselves they were in a war between God and Satan. Trying to save the world from evil, Wyatt felt he had to fight the devil to the death.

> Wyatt eventually accepted a plea deal where he was sentenced to 50 years and up to life in prison for murder.

The drug thing turned out much better for Dock Ellis than for Jarrod Wyatt.

HOGGING THE ATTENTION

Sporting events, seemingly more often in baseball than other professional sports, regularly engineer fan friendly shows on the field. A short break from the action takes place, hopefully to make people laugh. Often prizes are given.

During a May 2006 baseball game in Mexico, the comedy was ratcheted up when a planned event ran amok. A pig had been brought to the premises as part of a fan promotion but escaped from its handlers and began running laps around the diamond. Although not to be confused with a thoroughbred racehorse, the pig stayed ahead of human pursuers for some time.

It was never clear if the pig was going to slide at home plate, but it didn't make it before being intercepted. The team's chicken mascot set up a roadblock when it removed the chicken head and threw it at the pig. Of course, this broke the cardinal rule of mascot acting by going out of character, but it was an emergency.

THE DEATH OF RAY CHAPMAN

Major League Baseball got its start with the creation of the National League in 1876. It has been going strong for more than 140 years, called the National Pastime in American Society, and acknowledged as the best baseball league in the universe, attracting top players from other nations as well as the best American players.

In all of that time, just 1 player of the approximately 18,000 baseball individuals who have files in the National Baseball Hall of Fame Research Library in Cooperstown, New York, has been killed on the field of play.

> On August 16, 1920, the Cleveland Indians faced the New York Yankees at the Polo Grounds. Ray Chapman started at shortstop for Cleveland. He was batting .303 and a main reason the Indians led a close American League pennant race ahead of the Yankees.

Chapman, 29, was in his 9th season with the big club and over the previous few seasons had blossomed into a fairly steady .300

hitter. He was batting 2nd in the order for that game and was 0-for-1 after his first at-bat. Pitching for the Yankees was right-hander Carl Mays, who was known for his irascible personality and his style of throwing what was called a submarine pitch because it was hurled with an underhand motion.

Mays was extremely effective and on his way to a 26-victory season, 1 of the highest win totals in baseball that year. The pitch that killed Chapman was a fastball that Mays said was thrown high and caught Chapman as he was leaning over the plate, smacking him right in the head with such force that people within 100 feet of the batter's box claimed they heard a terrible thud.

Chapman fell to his knees, and blood began spurting in the area of his left ear. The plate umpire was Tommy Connelly, and he immediately began yelling for a doctor. Chapman appeared to be attempting to sit up, and those rushing to the plate began treating his wound with ice. From initial unconsciousness, Chapman came to. A very popular player, the Indians were extremely concerned about his fate, with good reason, as it turned out.

Chapman actually rose to his feet and began leaving the field under his own power. The team's clubhouse was in centerfield, not behind the dugout, as is common today. As he was passing 2nd base, Chapman began to collapse. Teammates grabbed him and carried him off the field in front of a horrified crowd of about 20,000 fans.

Taken to St. Lawrence Hospital for treatment, Chapman underwent surgery. However, he was pronounced dead at 4:40 a.m., about 12 hours after he was struck. Chapman's wife, Kathleen, pregnant with the couple's first child, rushed to New York but arrived after his death. Chapman was then transported to Cleveland for a very public funeral.

> After the 1920 season, Major League Baseball outlawed several kinds of oddball pitches, including the spitball (though practitioners were grandfathered in), trying to make the game safer and to increase offense.

In the near century since, numerous other hitters suffered egregious injuries from being hit in the head by pitched balls, and many pitchers have been struck in the head by line drives during games. However, no other player has ever died as a direct result of a play on the field of play.

It was not until 1956, after Little League took a similar step, that the National League required those coming to the plate to wear batting helmets. Two years later, the American League initiated the same requirement.

THE DEATH OF BILL MASTERSON

A player for the Minnesota North Stars, Bill Masterson is the only National Hockey League player to die directly from injuries sustained on the ice.

Masterson was a center just shy of his 30th birthday who broke into the NHL in 1961 with the Montreal Canadiens after a stellar career at the University of Denver. Masterson was a star for 2 Pioneers teams that won NCAA championships—and he earned an engineering degree from the school. However, he did not get a real chance in the NHL until the league expanded from 6 teams to 12 in 1967. He scored the 1st goal in North Stars team history.

On January 13, 1968, Masterson was skating for the North Stars in a game against the Oakland Seals when he took a hard hit on ice and suffered massive head injuries. Masterson incurred brain trauma during the Met Center game when Oakland players Larry Cahan and Ron Harris converged on him rushing up ice.

Masterson had just passed the puck away when the opposing players collided with him. Masterson fell backward to the ice, hitting his head on the hard sheet. Masterson was knocked unconscious before he hit the ice, and after his head bounced on the ice, he began bleeding from his nose, ears, and mouth. Those nearby said they saw Masterson briefly come awake and say, "Never again. Never again." He then lost consciousness again.

Although Masterson was rushed to the hospital for treatment and doctors examined him, they felt his injury was so severe they could not perform surgery. Masterson died 2 days later after being removed from life support with his wife and family members at his bedside.

It was later said that Masterson had suffered from previous concussions that could have made him more susceptible to the catastrophic head injury that killed him.

Masterson's death was so dramatic it sparked some early debate on the advisability of hockey players wearing helmets at all times on the ice. A few players chose to do so, but another 11 years passed before the league made the head gear mandatory.

The Professional Hockey Writers Association established The Bill Masterson Memorial Trophy at the end of the 1968 season. It is awarded to the NHL player "who best exemplifies the qualities of perseverance, sportsmanship, and dedication to hockey."

In 1985, Masterson was selected for the Colorado Sports Hall of Fame for his superb play at the University of Denver. In 1997, he was chosen for the 50th anniversary NCAA team.

THE DEATH OF HANK GATHERS

In 1990, Hank Gathers was 1 of the finest players in college basketball. The 6-foot-7, 210-pound forward was a star for Loyola Marymount. Just 23, he seemed destined for National Basketball Association stardom until he shocked America when he keeled over during a West Coast Conference tournament game against the Portland Pilots and died from a previously diagnosed heart condition.

Only a few months earlier, on December 9, 1989, Gathers had collapsed at a home game against University of California-Santa Barbara. He underwent tests and was determined to have an abnormal heartbeat. He was placed on medication but said his body did not respond well to it. Gathers felt he could not play like himself. Gradually, the medication was reduced, and he seemed to thrive again.

Gathers went down on the court during the first half of the Portland game and stopped breathing. Soon after, he was pronounced dead at a local Los Angeles hospital.

Family members filed lawsuits for negligence and were awarded separate million-dollar-plus awards.

THE DEATH OF LEN BIAS

A talented All-American forward out of the University of Maryland, Len Bias was the No. 1 draft pick of the Boston Celtics of the NBA on June 17, 1986, the league's second overall pick. The Celtics were counting on Bias to become a key part of the future for an aging team.

Two days later, in a development that stunned the nation, Bias died from cardiac arrhythmia, a result of a cocaine overdose. Many said Bias was never known to take drugs, and others said he was celebrating his good fortune in being selected by the Celtics.

It was revealed that Bias took cocaine with some friends at his dorm for several hours on the night he passed away. Three of those friends were indicted by a grand jury for possession of cocaine and possession of cocaine with intent to distribute. Charges were dropped against 2 of them for testimony against the 3rd, but that friend was acquitted.

In a shake-up subsequent to Bias's death, the University of Maryland athletic director and basketball coach resigned.

NOBODY IN THE HOUSE

On April 29, 2015, the Baltimore Orioles and Chicago White Sox played a Major League Baseball game at Camden Yards with an attendance of 0. Fans were forbidden to attend the contest because Baltimore was staggering through a period of civil unrest in the streets.

However, the game went on under all of the usual rules, and the Orioles were victors, 8–2. Various players got into the strange atmosphere. Baltimore catcher Caleb Joseph pantomimed signing autographs for nonexistent fans. When a bat flew out of a hitter's hands, a ball girl picked it up and pretended to hand it to a kid in the stands.

" The scoreboard told the game's story, as usual. Songs were played as if fans were on hand to enjoy them. And the game counted in the American League standings. "

CHAPTER 4
WEIRD SPORTS QUOTES

Former Chicago White Sox manager Ozzie Guillen is a native of Venezuela. A solid Major League player, Guillen was known for his outspoken and often humorous comments in 2005 as he led the Sox to their first World Series title since 1917. "The Venezuelan people that know me don't feel proud because we're winning," Guillen said. "They're proud because they go, 'How can this crazy man be the leader of a team?'"

Widely known as an avid baseball aficionado, actress Tallulah Bankhead once offered a make-them-pause cross-cultural comparison. "There have been only 2 authentic geniuses in the world," Bankhead said. "Willie Mays and Willie Shakespeare."

Charlez Schulz, the revered cartoonist who created the *Peanuts* comic strip, often included baseball comments in his work, especially as applied to Charlie Brown. This sounds very much like what any of his children might say: "Beethoven can't really be great because his picture isn't on a bubblegum card."

> Once upon a time, Northern Ireland's George Best was 1 of the best soccer players in the world for Manchester United. There seems little doubt he had a lot of fun fulfilling that role. "I spent 90 percent of my money on women and drink," Best said. "The rest I wasted."

Pedro Guerrero was once a fine Major League hitter who played parts of 15 seasons in the big leagues. Sometimes it bothered him more what he read about himself in a newspaper than making outs at-bat. "Sometimes they write what I say, not what I mean," said

Guerrero in referring to baseball scribes, when perhaps he should have been talking to Sigmund Freud.

———

Back to the genius category, former National Football League quarterback Joe Theismann did not do his research before uttering a memorable comment. "Nobody in football should be called a genius," Theismann said, no doubt in response to a trend some years back to call many pro coaches, geniuses. "A genius is a guy like Norman Einstein." Or perhaps his distant cousin Albert, of whom it is a little-known fact he was once a late draft pick of the Detroit Lions.

———

While Charles Barkley was a Hall of Fame professional basketball player and many consider him to be an all-world announcer, it seems unlikely he will be nominated for the Salesman Hall of Fame. Like so many other hoopsters, Barkley's name was slapped on a brand of sneaker that presumably would make the buyer Be Like Chuck. Unless you listened to his pitch. "These are my new shoes," Barkley said. "They're good shoes. They won't make you rich like me. They won't make you rebound like me. They definitely won't make you handsome like me. They'll only make you have shoes like me. That's it."

———

When pitcher Bill Lee was playing for the Boston Red Sox and Montreal Expos, he gained the nickname "Spaceman." That's because many people believed he was really way out there. The reality was Lee was simply wittier and more of an outside-the-box thinker than others in baseball. The 1960s was a wild time in the United States, the generation of free love and marijuana smoking, long hair and government protests. Lee fit right in. "The other day they asked me about drug testing (in baseball decades after his playing career)," Lee said. "I said I believed in drug testing a long time ago. All through the 60s, I tested everything."

Professional sports teams have sponsored special giveaways at selected games for decades, often a ball- or bat night in baseball, or a puck night in hockey. One night, the New York Rangers gave away team mugs for a game at Madison Square Garden. That may have seemed an innocent promotion, but things turned ugly when fans began hurling the cups onto the ice. "I'm just glad it wasn't Machete Night," said New York goaltender Bob Froese.

Gregg Popovich has been a long-time, very successful coach of the San Antonio Spurs in the National Basketball Association. Sometimes he likes to tweak sportswriters with responses to questions. Other times, he may make political statements that have nothing to do with the just-played game. And still other times, he may just say something to surprise people. "Any other incisive, deep questions that make my mind go vertiginous?" he said in a postgame press conference. "None of you even know what that means." The context was being asked if just playing a close game might have been good for his team after it had won many others by large margins. A quick interpretation, without looking up vertiginous in the dictionary, probably would have been "No."

Golden State Warriors All-Star Kevin Durant was asked to evaluate young New York Knicks player Kristaps Porzingis. "He's a skilled player," Durant said. "He's like a unicorn." That could well be the first time the word "unicorn" appeared in a National Basketball Association scouting report.

At best, people only thought they knew what gonzo journalist Hunter S. Thompson meant when he uttered the phrase "When the going gets weird, the weird turn pro." But regardless of the comprehension level, it caught on anyway, and decades later people still repeat it.

Buffalo Sabres hockey star Gilbert Perreault made a statement that very much had the ring of truth to it once it was pondered. In fact, it has the staying power that makes it as accurate today as it was years ago. Perreault said, "The 3 most important elements in hockey are the forecheck, the back-check, and the paycheck." Just ask around.

College football coach Mike Leach, most recently the leader at Washington State University, has never been shy about voicing his thoughts, much to the enjoyment of sportswriters. He observes that the United States seems to become erratically obsessed about things that should rate very low on the importance scale. He made this comment when a football scandal involving the New England Patriots and Tom Brady was labeled Deflategate. "With everything that's going on," Leach said, "we're worried about how much air goes into a ball, when everybody uses their own ball. It's like it's a forged football. We waste a lot of time with that, and then we worry about the Kardashians. How can it be that we laugh about England's obsession with the royal family? At least the royal family has college degrees and military service."

Phil Mickelson is a great golfer with a long record of success, and he seemed to be sincere when he made the following comment. We sort of figured out what he meant when he said, "I owe a lot to my parents, especially my mother and father."

When the player first joined the NBA his name was Ron Artest Jr. He subsequently changed his name to Metta World Peace. There aren't many people named Peace in the phone book. One reason to change his name thus, he said, is "I'm a big fan of the Nobel Peace Prize." Aren't we all?

> It wasn't clear how the naming would go, but another former NBA player, Chuck Nevitt, befuddled listeners when he informed them, "My sister's expecting a baby and I don't know if I'm going to be an aunt or an uncle." Pretty much everyone else was sure, though.

Basketball star Tracy McGrady may have gone to summer school for a geography course during his pro career, and it seemingly paid off. Just ask him. "My career was sputtering until I did a 360 and got headed in the right direction," he said. He did not say if that was north, south, east, or west.

MUHAMMAD ALI

If there was a talking Hall of Fame, Muhammad Ali would be a member. Instead, he had to settle for the Boxing Hall of Fame. Many people believe Ali invented trash talking in sports, and while that is not literally true, it might as well be. The former heavyweight champion of the world was a brash, outgoing motormouth who issued humorous 1-liners like a standup comedian. He had no governor on his tongue and he had no interest in placing 1 on it.

When Ali was very young, still called Cassius Clay, and back home in Kentucky after winning an Olympic medal in the 1960 Olympics in Rome, he made an appearance at a radio station. Also present was the famous, fabulous wrestler Gorgeous George. Fueled by his own blabbermouth, decked out in colorful flowing robes, and visible from afar because of his own dyed platinum hair, Gorgeous George virtually created an era of show business professional wrestling.

Gorgeous George thrived on controversy, people loving or hating him, flashy dressing, offbeat gimmicks, and making outrageous statements. All of those habits drew bushels of attention to him and made him a superstar of ticket sales for live shows. Not only did Gorgeous George pass on advice to Ali, but Ali absorbed the sensation the wrestler caused, and some of the act rubbed off on him.

Until Ali burst upon the sporting scene in the early 1960s, most athletes were seen as aw-shucks types who toed the line, non-controversial, and god-awful boring. Ali altered the landscape, set a different bar of behavior. He irritated some and made others laugh, often at the same time, because he wasn't always polite. But everyone knew who he was. Ali made irreverent boasts about how he was going to knock the block off a specific fighter, stunningly even predicting in what round he was going to score a knockout. The thing about Ali was that he could back up his big talk.

> Muhammad Ali uttered so many weird and wondrous things, often in poetry, it was hard to keep up. His greatest hits would fill a volume of the encyclopedia.

"It's hard to be humble when you're as great as I am," was 1 of Ali's frequent statements that registered across the spectrum of reaction.

"I'm so mean, I make medicine sick" was 1 thing Ali said that was hard to figure out.

———

"I shook up the world. Me! Whee!" That was true of Ali so many times.

———

"I've wrestled with alligators, I've tussled with a whale. I done handcuffed lightning. And thrown thunder in jail." There is no physical evidence Ali grappled with a whale. The rest could be true.

———

"I'm the most recognized and loved man that ever lived cuz there weren't no satellites when Jesus and Moses were around, so people far away in the villages didn't know about them."

> Just in case word had not reached all of the corners of the planet, Ali was always good for a reminder of just what he thought about himself.

When he was alive and in his prime, it was often said Muhammad Ali possessed the most recognized face in the world.

PRO-WRESTLING 1-LINERS

Pro wrestling surrendered in its fight to be referred to as a sport when it changed from the World Wrestling Federation to World Wrestling Entertainment after losing a court battle with the World Wildlife Fund for the right to use the initials WWF.

Over the decades, wrestling went all in on show business as a counterbalance to the sports-only image, and as a result, it mushroomed in popularity on television, on closed circuit TV, and online. Wrestlers were encouraged to become more outrageous, and that often resulted in increasingly astonishing comments.

In some cases, those blurt-out statements were witty, amazing, and insulting.

Jerry Lawler, whose nickname is "The King," was long the king of the Memphis area wrestling shows, and he displayed an acerbic wit during his TV commentary. On many occasions, he referred to older participants as if they had been around since the Garden of Eden.

Of Helen Hart, matriarch of the Hart wrestling family who died in 2001, Lawler offered a double whammy, "Helen Hart is the only person I know with an autographed copy of the Bible."

Also, he said, "Helen Hart is so old she remembers when the Dead Sea was sick."

> Lawler also dissed Alundra Blayze, who was a wrestler known as Medusa.

"You know, Alundra Blayze, with her looks could star in TV westerns . . . if she had 2 more legs," Lawler said.

The wrestler known as The Rock, who has become even better known as actor Dwayne Johnson, knew how to play the banter game when he was combating wrestling opponents. He often spoke in the third person as an ego thing. Before facing 1 foe, he said, "The Rock says this, if the Rock hits you, he'll kill you. If he misses, the wind behind the punch will give you pneumonia and you'll die anyway, so the choice is yours, jabroni."

Jim Cornette, podcaster and sometime pro wrestler who was not as well known as the target of his insult, expressed his intense feelings about Hulk Hogan: "And on a personal note to Hulk

Hogan, you are a household word, but so is garbage, and it stinks when it gets old, too."

Jesse Ventura parlayed his fame as a professional wrestler into a temporary job as governor of Minnesota. After practicing slick moves, he practiced political moves. Explaining how he could appear as a bad guy by the growth of facial hair, Ventura said, "In wrestling, my mustache made me look more like a villain. A good mustache can give you the look of the devil." From professional wrestling fame to governor of a state! That may be the weirdest career promotion in sports history.

Prominent grappler Chris Jericho, winner of many championships, found a way to compare professional wrestling and dancing, though he did not specifically mention ballet. "There are a lot of similarities between dancing and wrestling," Jericho said. "The costumes are the same, the spandex and all that, but you have to be light on your feet to do both, and you have to remember choreography." Jericho, also a professional heavy metal singer, managed to express himself in dance on *Dancing with the Stars* during season 12 in 2011.

NONE OF THE UMPIRES ARE MY BEST FRIENDS

Fans of a committed persuasion have never been very patient with the officials who call infractions on the teams of their choice.

Going back way, the phrase "Kill the umpire" was often employed by disgruntled supporters at Major League baseball games.

Johnny Evers, the ill-tempered but talented Hall of Fame second baseman, was known for his determination and desire to win. He did not have much sympathy for the umpiring profession, either.

> He once made a comment about where he stood on the arbiters of the game. "My favorite umpire is a dead one," Evers said.

THE SARCASTIC TRUTH

John McKay was a terrific football coach, leading the University of Southern California to collegiate glory. Feeling he had accomplished all he could at that level of the game, and no doubt also lured by big bucks, McKay took a flyer. In 1976, he signed on to be the first coach of the expansion Tampa Bay Buccaneers of the National Football League. What he did not realize initially was that he had signed on without a parachute.

McKay presided over the worst team in pro football history—and he did not keep quiet about it. The Bucs lost their first 26 games before eking out a victory. McKay was not a rah-rah guy. If he saw something that he hated on the field, he did not keep his emotions inside.

Postgame press conferences were hard to take for McKay because the games had been a series of awful minitragedies. Once, when asked, "What did you think of your team's execution?" McKay said, "I'm in favor of it."

McKay compared coaching an expansion team to a religious experience. "You do a lot of praying, but most of the time the answer is no."

Most weeks after a defeat, you could pick your shortcoming as a way to describe things the Bucs did poorly. Once, McKay said, "We did not tackle well today, but we made up for it by not blocking."

During the period when the Bucs were losing every game, they became a regular punch line on *The Tonight Show Starring Johnny Carson*; Carson was even wittier than McKay, but he didn't have to watch every Tampa Bay game.

Carson sometimes played a mystical swami figure named Carnac and 1 night, he responded to a quiz challenge ordering him to "name 2 natural disasters that were accompanied by band music." The answer? "The Titanic and the Buccaneers."

BASEBALL CHATTER

Tug McGraw, an exceptional relief pitcher for the New York Mets and Philadelphia Phillies, and fellow reliever Al Holland, a team-mate in Philadelphia, used to enjoy bantering in the bullpen awaiting the call from a manager to come into the game and save a starter.

> Both were known for being light-hearted, fun-loving fellows and seemed to acknowledge it.

"I talk to Tug McGraw in the bullpen all the time," Holland said. "Neither of us has an elevator that goes to the top floor, so mostly we talk from the waist down."

SEEMS LIKE A COMPLIMENT

Phil Niekro won 318 games in the majors and is a member of the Baseball Hall of Fame. His bread-and-butter weapon was the knuckleball. The dipsy-doodle pitch that has always baffled even the best of hitters when its practitioner is on has also often defied description.

When Bobby Murcer, the 1-time New York Yankees outfielder, began discussing the effectiveness of Niekro's knuckler, it wasn't clear if he was talking baseball or the culinary arts.

"Trying to hit Phil Niekro," Murcer said, "is like trying to eat Jell-O with chopsticks." Do they make you come early to spring training to perfect that skill?

AND HE WASN'T EVEN HIT IN THE HEAD

Former heavyweight champion George Foreman experienced 2 completely different careers in boxing. The first followed his Olympic triumph as a young man when he was the most feared man on the planet, intimidating opponents not only with his fists, but his scowl.

After a 10-year retirement, Foreman made an unlikely successful comeback, this time as an underdog who charmed fans and opponents. It was a long trail back, and 1 of Foreman's opponents was a witty fellow named Frank "Gator" Williams.

———

Their bout in Anchorage, Alaska, ended abruptly with a Foreman knockout punch, not to the jaw or such a region, but with a body shot that moved Williams about 6 feet toward the center of the ring. The pain was sufficient that Williams could not continue.

———

Afterward, Williams said, "George Foreman hits so hard, he shakes your family tree."

DO WE DETECT ANIMOSITY HERE?

Shannon Sharpe was a Pro Football Hall of Fame tight end. Ray Lewis was a Hall of Fame linebacker. Often enough, they intersected where the ball showed up, Lewis the hitter and Sharpe the hittee.

> "Given Sharpe's outlook on Lewis, they did not appear to leave the gridiron as buddies."

"Ray Lewis is the type of guy, if he were in a fight with a bear, I wouldn't help him," Sharpe said. "I would pour honey on him because he likes to fight. That's the type of guy Ray Lewis is."

———

Obviously, Sharpe and Lewis were not destined to become tag-team wrestling partners. It's a bit murky here what is meant by the kind of guy Lewis is in fighting, but it seems apparent from the "pour honey" part of the equation, Sharpe would be rooting for the bear.

CARL EVERETT'S WAY OF LOOKING AT THINGS

Carl Everett was a solid-hitting Major League outfielder who had a lifetime batting average of .271 over 14 seasons with 8 teams. But if it wasn't about hitting, not everyone understood what Everett was talking about when he issued a soliloquy.

———

Although he was a baseball player, it definitely wasn't clear Everett had baseball on his mind when he uttered a peculiar thought 1 day. It most assuredly wasn't about the hit-and-run when he said, "God created the sun, the stars, and the earth, and then made Adam and Eve. The Bible never says anything about dinosaurs. You can't say there were dinosaurs when you never saw them. Someone actually saw Adam and Eve. No ever saw a Tyrannosaurus Rex." Perhaps it would have been best if Everett stuck to the Bible of Baseball, the Baseball Encyclopedia, the King Babe version.

DID THEY GO TO SCHOOL TOGETHER?

Mike Cameron, another reputable outfielder with some significant hitting achievements to his credit, including being 1 of those who share the big-league record for swatting 4 home runs in 1 game, may have taken the same science correspondence course as Everett.

> "The sun has been there for 500, 600 years," Cameron said.

Apparently before that, nobody had to wear shades.

AND HE COULD DUNK, TOO

Former National Basketball Association forward Charles Shackelford, who had his biggest court success for North Carolina State and in Europe, and who alas died young at 40, seemed to know his left from his right, but not necessarily his vocabulary. Once, in describing his dexterity in making moves to the basket, Shackelford invented a fresh way of looking at things. "I can go right, I can go left, I'm amphibious," he said.

Shackelford surely meant he was ambidextrous, which of course was not an accurate way of noting his talents using both hands well. Perhaps he needed a blinker to turn right or left?

GIVE HIM A MAP

Once, former heavyweight champion Mike Tyson was asked what he was likely to do when he retired from the ring. Apparently thinking about the loss of stardom and being in the public eye, Tyson said, "Fade into Bolivian, I guess."

Many a star has faded into oblivion, but not many have taken refuge in Bolivia. If Tyson had adopted a noble mission, he could have undergone a search for Butch Cassidy and the Sundance Kid, since according to movie lore that is where they were last seen.

NEEDS A REFRESHER IN JEWISH LAW

Long before New England Patriots Coach Bill Belichick was accused of breaking National Football League rules, onetime Pittsburgh Steelers Head Coach Bill Cowher felt compelled to defend himself and his squad against accusations that he was trying to tiptoe around some rules. "We're not attempting to circumcise rules," Cowher said.

No. 1, that should have made all baby boys within reach feel better. No. 2, was that a denial, an obfuscation, or a just a slick way out of getting out of an answer? Just like those rules he wasn't circumventing, or circumnavigating.

KING OF NIGHTLIFE

Hall of Fame center Shaquille O'Neal was a great basketball player in his heyday, but apparently, he was a Hall of Fame nightclub visitor, too.

After a trip to Greece, O'Neal was making chitchat with reporters and was asked what he did on the trip to the ancient country, as in Did he see the sights like the Parthenon?

> "I can't really remember the names of all the clubs we went to," O'Neal said.

Maybe there really was a nightclub called The Parthenon that was a hot spot.

ANOTHER BIBLICAL MIXUP

At different times in his football coaching career, Ron Meyer was head man at Southern Methodist University, in charge of the New England Patriots, and leader of the Indianapolis Colts.

Meyer had a considerable amount of success as a coach. He took over the Colts when the team was 0–13 and won 3 straight games, considered a minimiracle. The next season, the Colts made the playoffs.

When Meyer was asked if he could lead the Colts to the Promised Land, presumably, the Super Bowl in National Football League parlance, he stuck to the theme and answered in religious terms—sort of—indicating there might be limitations.

"It's not like we came down from Mount Sinai with the tabloids," he said.

Who knew the *National Enquirer* had a printing press on Mount Sinai?

HE LIKED TO SCORE ANY WAY HE COULD

Antoine Walker was a star at the University of Kentucky and in the NBA. He was a 6-foot-9, 245-pound forward. He embraced the

3-point shot earlier than many other forwards, even though some observers felt with his size he could obtain higher percentage shots from closer to the basket.

Walker was neither ashamed, nor abashed, about his shot selection, and when he was asked why he attempted so many shots from beyond the arc, he had a ready answer.

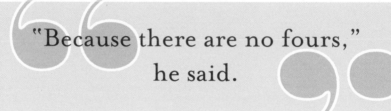

"Because there are no fours," he said.

Undoubtedly, Walker would have been happy to heave from 30 feet rather than pausing at 22 feet.

CHAPTER 5
WEIRD SPORTS NICKNAMES

PRO BASEBALL PLAYERS

Bill Lee was a very good left-handed pitcher for the Boston Red Sox and Montreal Expos, but he was probably even a funnier guy. Lee was always on his own program, looking at the world through eyes that easily recognized absurdity.

That meant that he was not easily tamed and often delivered comments that made stuffed shirts recoil. As a result, even teammates thought he was a bit far out there. Far out there, as in outer space, so Lee was given the nickname "Spaceman." He was no astronaut, but he flummoxed other players with statements that seemed to come from galaxies far, far away.

Although being called a spaceman was often said with malice, Lee was not the least bit offended. Once, he said of being given such a label, "Everybody thinks they're earthlings, but in actuality, we're here only for a brief moment."

> So there. You weren't going to catch Lee being too serious about playing a little boy's game.

You had to stretch to consider Jim Grant's nickname of Mudcat to be a sincere compliment, especially knowing what was behind it. Grant was the first African American to win a World Series game for an American League team and won 145 regular-season games during his career.

The Mudcat appellation was added to his given name by Hall of Famer Larry Doby, who presumably provided it as a term of endearment, though in a trash-talking manner. He said he called Grant Mudcat because he was "as ugly as a Mississippi mudcat."

This was a nickname that stuck like Super Glue. These days if you mention Jim Grant, nobody will know who you're talking about, but if you say Jim "Mudcat" Grant, it is crystal clear.

Jim Hunter was a Hall of Fame pitcher for the Oakland Athletics and New York Yankees who made it through a good portion of his career without the nickname of "Catfish." Eccentric A's owner Charlie Finley decided it would be cool to give someone with the last name of Hunter a nickname relating to fishing. Finley felt it would provide valuable publicity and color.

Finley went to work creating fiction. Not only was he the originator of the nickname, he was also the author of the story that supposedly led to the bestowing of the nickname. The fabricated story was that as a youth, Hunter had run away from his farm home, and when he was found, he was toting 2 catfish he caught. Up until then, Hunter was better known as Jimmy.

The winningest pitcher of all time, Denton True Young came off a farm in Ohio where his fastball was supposedly so fast that it broke boards in a wooden fence. In exclamation, an observer said he threw as fast as a cyclone. Eventually, the description of a strong windstorm like that was shortened to the diminutive of Cy.

Cy, of course, meant nothing at all as a first name. It was neither Young's true first name nor really reminded folks of the original cyclone nickname. In the end, practically no baseball fans recall the winner of 511 games having the first name of Denton. Everyone called him Cy.

———

Hall of Fame pitcher Dazzy Vance also dazzled with his fastball, but that had nothing to do with his nickname. Born Clarence Arthur, Vance became addicted to the flavorful expression "Ain't that a daisy?" Movie buffs will recall that the Doc Holliday character in the movie *Tombstone* played by Val Kilmer regularly used that phrase.

> The difference between Kilmer's pronunciation and that of Vance, who was born in Homosassa Springs, Florida, is that Vance pronounced daisy as Dazzy. So that's who he became.

Carl Furillo was a top-notch outfielder for the Brooklyn and Los Angeles Dodgers in the late 1940s and 1950s, particularly admired for his strong arm. He was from an area of Pennsylvania near Reading, and because of that power in his right arm, he was nicknamed "The Reading Rifle." That one made sense.

———

Furillo had another nickname as well, and unless you knew him at the time, few understood it. And since Furillo's death in 1989, probably no future baseball fans have any idea what is being talked about when the alternative nickname is brought up unless they are from Italy. That nickname was "Skoonj." Furillo had a strong fondness for scungilli, or conches, his favorite food. He must have eaten a lot of them to get such a nickname.

———

Jim Wynn was a very reliable offensive outfielder for the Houston Astros in the 1960s. By baseball standards he was not a large man, measuring 5-foot-9 and 160 pounds. Yet he was able to hit with good power. That trait led to the creation of his nickname by a Texas sportswriter.

———

Wynn became known as the "Toy Cannon." He very much had mixed feelings about it when it was first applied. It called attention to Wynn's short stature, but it was given as a compliment to how he packed so much hitting prowess into his frame.

———

Initially, to Wynn's dismay, the nickname spread like wildfire. Everyone was using it in sports articles and on game telecasts.

He couldn't duck it. Eventually, Wynn came to terms with the nickname as an identifier, and decades later when he wrote an autobiography, he used the nickname as the title of the book.

Probably not one in 100 baseball fans know the pitcher Preacher Roe's real first name. Checking out his birth certificate, a reader would discover his given name was Elwin Charles Roe. One must wonder if anyone but his mother used that name, and for a limited time only.

According to Roe's own mother, her little baby boy began calling himself Preacher when he was 3 years old. Seriously? A 3-year-old gives himself a nickname? How many 3-year-olds know their entire name, never mind running around calling themselves anything except Superman or Batman as an alternative?

That was her story, and she was sticking to it. It seems Roe developed a fondness for the local reverend, who was referred to in conversation as Preacher, so the kid adopted the nickname Preacher. Whether he prayed for divine assistance or not, Preacher Roe was selected to five All-Star teams and won 127 big-league games.

George Stirnweiss was a 2nd baseman for the New York Yankees in the 1940s. He probably did not seek out his peculiar nickname of "Snuffy," which sounded as if it were a refugee from the comics pages in newspapers.

Those in the know say Stirnweiss was given the nickname for 1 of 2 reasons. Either he was so overwhelmed by sniffling, or snuffing, due to allergies, or because he treated his sniffling with an abundance of snuff.

> Modern fans who hear about smokeless tobacco think of it only in terms of chewing tobacco. Snuff was inhaled as smokeless tobacco.

Hall of Fame outfielder Edwin Snider was one of the toasts of New York during the 1950s, when 3 ball clubs, the Yankees, Giants, and Brooklyn Dodgers each had star centerfielders. Snider joined Mickey Mantle and Willie Mays at the most exalted position of the era.

Snider was nicknamed Duke, but the odd thing was his nickname came from his youth, not because he was a baseball star on the big stage. His family called him that because as a little boy, he strutted around like royalty.

New York Giants manager John McGraw thought his dream of bringing a Jewish star to prominence in the big city had come true when he discovered Mose Hirsch Solomon, who was immediately nicknamed "The Rabbi of Swat." McGraw always believed a person who was Jewish would be besieged by fans because there were so many Jewish residents in New York looking for a hero.

> McGraw felt the need more keenly in the early 1920s, when Babe Ruth came upon the scene and transformed the New York Yankees from also-rans to champions with his home-run-hitting prowess. Their attendance totals mushroomed.

Solomon was a good athlete who was a boxing champ in Ohio under an assumed name, never mind a nickname, using Henry Sully. He also played football for the Carlisle Indian School with Jim Thorpe.

Ruth had made the home run a nuclear weapon in the game, and Solomon was a power hitter in the minors who in 1922 stroked a minor-league record 49 home runs in a single season for the Class C Hutchinson Wheat Shockers in Kansas. He did so in just 108 games while batting .421, an astounding season.

McGraw was looking for box office, as well as home-run prowess, and, forgetting the difference between Class C ball and the majors, gave Solomon a roster spot at the end of the 1923 season. The Babe was also known as "The Sultan of Swat," but "The Rabbi of Swat" didn't last. Despite a lifetime .375 average, going 3-for-8 in 2 games, Solomon was a dreadful fielder. He ended up back in the minors the next season, likely a designated hitter prospect playing in the wrong era. The nickname, though, was weird and wonderful.

It is not a pretty story, because Jack Lohrke received the nickname "Lucky" for deadly serious reasons. Lucky was alliterative with Lohrke, but that wasn't all. Lohrke was a Major League 3rd baseman between 1947 and 1953. To say he was fortunate to have played at all is a massive understatement and a remarkable testament to the quirks of life—and death.

Numerous times, Lohrke safely missed out on accidents that killed other people he had just been with or was next to. During World War II, Lohrke was traveling on a troop train that crashed and killed 3 soldiers while injuring others. During the D-Day invasion landing on Normandy Beach, in the Battle of the Bulge, and in other combat, 4 times soldiers next to Lohrke were killed.

> After the war ended and Lohrke was being mustered out, he could not immediately get all the way home to Los Angeles. He was scheduled to board a plane at Camp Pendleton but was bumped by someone of higher rank. That plane crashed, killing all passengers.

In 1946, Lohrke was playing AA baseball in the minors when his sterling performance gained him sufficient attention for a promotion. During that pre-cell phone era, there was no way to reach Lohrke to tell him to abandon his club and report immediately to a AAA team. Finally, when the team stopped at a coffee shop for dinner near Bremerton, Washington, the message he was being moved up a classification reached Lorhke.

———

Lohrke grabbed his gear and suitcase and began hitchhiking to Spokane, the closest big city, so he could make his way to San Diego by flight to greet his new team. After Lorhke left his Class B Spokane Indians, that team continued on without him. However, the bus had a serious accident, crashing through a guard rail on a mountain. Nine of the 15 players were killed in the crash.

———

The charmed life of Jack Lohrke came to an end in 2009, when he died of old age at 85. Lohrke received his nickname for surviving so many close calls and because he was so Lucky to do so.

PRO BASKETBALL PLAYERS

As always, some nicknames are funny, some are appropriate, some go beyond the bounds, and some sound just stupid enough to be examined and analyzed to the point the only response is "Huh?"

Jameer Nelson, the long-time National Basketball Association point guard, received what can only be viewed as an unwanted nickname from onetime teammate Dwight Howard. After all, who wants to have the name "Crib Midget" emblazoned on his bubble gum card, uniform, or tombstone?

> Nelson is 6 feet tall and weighs 190 pounds, so under no definition of the word *midget* is the nickname accurate. It's also difficult to figure out how it is laudatory or friendly, either. It's mostly a moniker that comes under the heading of Go Figure.

Interestingly, David Lee, a solid power forward, picked up a quirky nickname because he reminded some others of Dwight Howard despite being Caucasian. That nickname was "Da White Howard." Not sure that one is a compliment either, but it does have some cleverness behind it.

Joel Pryzbilla had a long career in the pros. No doubt his lon-gevity was aided by his size of 7-foot-1. This alone did not explain his nickname of "The Vanilla Gorilla," however. Was he an endan-gered species?

Back in 1989 and 1990, when the Detroit Pistons won back-to-back league championships, the group was nicknamed "The Bad Boys" for hard-nosed, or even in some minds dirty, play. You did not mess with the Pistons physically. They were tough under the boards and on defense. Two of the key protagonists were Rick Mahorn and Jeff Ruland. Their nicknames were actually brilliant for the moment, not as weird as many others, more apt than many. The duo was termed "McFilthy" and "McNasty." If you didn't like it, they made you lump it, or gave lumps.

The marvelously talented Shawn Marion could jump high and zoom past defenders. It was almost as if he could levitate. His smooth skills gained him the nickname "The Matrix," named after the 1999 science fiction film starring Keanu Reeves and others possessing super-perception powers. It was definitely a compli-ment to Marion in his prime.

Rafer Alston played six seasons in the NBA and had a very flaky nickname: "Skip to My Lou," a children's song. The song's origins date to the 1840s, and it was said to be a favorite of President Abraham Lincoln, though not because of American Top 40 programming. It was introduced as part of a game at dances signaling young adults to switch partners.

What's the connection to Alston? Good question. His playing style involved what has been described as herky-jerky moves, while dancing usually involves smooth moves. Did he pick up the nickname because he was good at stealing the basketball? In any case, Alston embraced it and even had the nickname applied to a shoe called the Skip to My Lou 2. Put on your dancing basketball shoes.

Lance Stephenson, who has had some quality seasons with the Indiana Pacers, has struggled playing for other NBA teams. There is no apparent reason why. But this inconsistency holds him back from living up to a nickname he earned when he was a phenom as a younger player. He was called "Born Ready," but he hasn't always been.

Darryl Dawkins probably had more fun playing professional basketball than anyone else in the history of the NBA. He was known for giving his various dunks nicknames, and no one did it better. Dawkins stood 6-foot-11, was a powerful man, was liked by all, and held down a mix of nicknames, including "Sir Slam" and "Dr. Dunkenstein." The best was "Chocolate Thunder." The man behind the nickname for Dawkins was singer Stevie Wonder, who was blind, so he couldn't even see Dawkins's best moves, but he surely must have been able to feel the vibes.

> Just because Tim Duncan was a terrific player as a championship forward for the San Antonio Spurs from 1997 to 2016 and his nickname is an accurate one, that doesn't mean it isn't weird. "The Big Fundamental"? Okay, Duncan was known for playing a very fundamentally sound game, but really, that nickname? Snore. And today, class, we will study the fundamentals.

Shaquille O'Neal was another Hall of Famer who prided himself on not only dominating the paint, but dominating conversations. He could be witty. He could be entertaining, but he amassed so many nicknames that he never acquired an iconic one. At various times, he was called "The Big Shamrock," "The Big Field General," "Superman," "The Diesel," and many more. Perhaps the best recalled is "The Big Aristotle." O'Neal fancied himself somewhat of a philosopher and pinned that nickname on himself.

In terms of weirdness, a new late-in-career nickname for guard Rajon Rondo is difficult to fathom. Rondo has had an excellent career as a point guard, but all of a sudden, announcers in Sacramento anointed him "The Yoga Instructor." Rondo has not taken a part-time job. Nor has he started taking yoga classes. The appendage to his name refers to Rondo being able to twist and turn while driving past defenders. That is too clever by half, not worthy of an enduring nickname.

To the average fan who knows of Australian guard Matthew Dellavedova, mention of the nickname "Outback Jesus" may cause confusion, or at the least a pause. What does it mean? It's easy enough to decipher the Outback part of the nickname just because Dellavedova brought his skills to the United States from Australia. He is from a small town called Maryborough, but it is located only a couple of hours' drive from Melbourne, so it isn't Crocodile Dundee outback.

Dellavedova could be called "Outback Jesus" because he is very religious, but you won't find much copy written about that. It could mean that some see him as a savior on the basketball court. Dellavedova himself seems to prefer the simpler nickname of "Delly," though some have called him the "Outback Assassin," which would be a testimony to his outside shot.

Corey Brewer was one of a gang of fine players who helped the University of Florida win 2 NCAA titles under Billy Donovan. Years later, he signed with the Oklahoma City Thunder, coached by Billy Donovan. Seemingly, Brewer put an embarrassing college nickname behind him since entering the pros. However, Donovan eventually revealed that once upon a time, Brewer was referred to as "The Drunken Dribbler." Some recall that before Brewer became a slicker ball handler, he had a propensity to trip and fall while dribbling. But no one survives more than a decade playing in the NBA if he is a klutz, making any attempt to revive the weird nickname seem silly.

A 7-time All-Star out of the University of Arkansas, forward Joe Johnson has always been able to score during his 17-year NBA playing career. He has been around and he has moved around and he has picked up nicknames on the way. One was "Iso-Joe" because he could play one-on-one. One was "Joe Jesus" because he likes to help people. "Big Shot Joe" came up because of Johnson's offense.

But the mind-boggler, with no apparent explanation, is "The Armadillo Cowboy." Say what?

> In the United States, the small, armor-plated animals are common in the Southwest. Johnson did play for Houston, so he does have some connection to the region, but there's no mention of him having a pet armadillo. He's not a cowboy with any rodeo or cattle ranching background. Johnson will just have to live with a nickname that makes no sense and that virtually nobody calls him.

PRO FOOTBALL PLAYERS

It is fascinating when 2 areas that might seem contradictory actually overlap in a good way. In this case, the first-rate wide receiver named Elroy Hirsch gained a nickname that is both weird and kind of neat at the same time.

A member of the Pro Football Hall of Fame and the College Football Hall of Fame, Hirsch was called "Crazylegs." It probably should have been 2 words, Crazy Legs, but for some reason was not. His less than smooth style of running in the open field is what gave Hirsch the nickname.

Hirsch was a terrific pass catcher who collected 387 throws during his career and was known as a big-play receiver as well, going for long yardage and touchdowns on a disproportionately high percentage of his receptions. He was fleet and shifty, and those crazy legs outran defenders regularly for the University of Wisconsin, the University of Michigan, the Chicago Rockets of the All-America Football Conference, and the Los Angeles Rams.

Chad Johnson was a colorful wide receiver, mostly for the Cincinnati Bengals, a game-breaker of a pass catcher. He was also a world-class talker who liked attention and discovered a new way to obtain it. One day, Johnson decided his last name was too tame, so he decided to do something about it. He trotted out for a game wearing the last name "Ochocinco" on the back of his jersey, but quarterback Carson Palmer ripped off the name tag, and Johnson played as Johnson. The NFL fined him $5,000 for the maneuver, but eventually Johnson informed sportswriters he had legally changed his last name to Ochocinco.

———

This was supposed to mean 85 in Spanish, although the literal translation was 8 and 5. Nobody much cared about that technicality, and Chad achieved his desired effect of adopting an unusual name that drew attention. After retirement, Johnson did return to being called Johnson, at least legally.

> While he went around telling everyone his name was Ochocinco, Johnson kept wearing Johnson on the back of his jersey during games. He said that was because of an endorsement contract with Reebok.

Continuing to tinker and fool around with the media, Johnson test-drove another metamorphosis, announcing he was going to change his name again, this time to "Hatchi Go," the equivalent of 85 in Japanese. That was a one-off, however, and he did not proceed to officially make that change.

All of this took place between 2006 and 2012. In 2012, when Johnson became property of the Miami Dolphins, he changed his legal name back to Chad Johnson.

The terrific James Harrison, who is the all-time leader in sacks for the Pittsburgh Steelers, was given the nickname "Deebo" because he reminded teammates of a movie character. In the film *Friday* and its sequels, a bully plays a significant part. Harrison pushed people around on defense the way "Deebo" pushed people around on the screen.

Another Harrison nickname, performance specific, was "Mr. Monday Night," because he always seemed to shine on *Monday Night Football* telecasts.

Walter Payton was one of the greatest football players in National Football League history. A fabulous running back who did not shy away from doing the dirty work, blocking and tackling, when thrust into those situations, he was widely respected for his work ethic and performance.

It always seemed odd that Payton's main nickname was "Sweetness," because he was not so sweet on the gridiron. Off the field, Payton was less hard-core, more of a nice guy, but "Sweetness" kind of overdid it. Payton appeared to embrace the nickname with an explanation, saying when not smacking into bigger, tough guys he liked to dance and romance. Maybe. Still seemed like a stretch for a football nickname.

> The marvelous ESPN sports announcer Chris Berman established as his trademark an ability to label players with creative nicknames, some of which were weird, some hilarious, and some a real reach. Generally, Berman was good at it, and many times a nickname stuck forever.

One of Berman's all-time memorable nicknames was given to Hall of Fame running back Curtis Martin of the Patriots and Jets, whom he dubbed "My Favorite Martian." That was a hit television show in the early 1960s. Martin and Martian sounded enough alike, and neither the football player nor the Martian (Ray Walston) was very tall for what they did.

Dick Lane played for the Los Angeles Rams, Chicago Cardinals, and Detroit Lions in the 1950s and 1960s and is regarded as one of the greatest cornerbacks who ever lived. A tenacious defender, Lane had just one major flaw, though it did not relate specifically to the football field.

Unable to cope with his dreaded fear of flying, Lane refused to travel to away games with the rest of his teams because they journeyed by jet. Instead, Lane traveled on his own to other cities by train. His nickname, "Night Train," was so ubiquitously used, many people didn't know his real first name.

Another Hall of Fame great, defensive back Brian Dawkins, acquired a nickname that could only stick by repeated application, because it has nothing to do with his real name or anything but his sterling, rugged style of play. "Weapon X" sounds more like a secret chemical compound.

However, Dawkins had a special connection to Wolverine, a premier Marvel Comics and movie character. He loved the guy, collecting Wolverine memorabilia and action figures and placing much of it on display in his Philadelphia Eagles locker. Also, it was almost as if Dawkins had a secret identity like Superman's Clark Kent, meek and mild and soft-spoken in civilian clothes, and then a killer character on the field once donning his football uniform. He called his game transformation persona "Weapon X."

> When Dawkins was retiring in 2012, the Eagles and Marvel conspired to develop a giveaway poster of him as "Weapon X."

Adrian Peterson is just about wrapping up his career as a top running back, but when he was younger, in his prime, and on the roster of the Minnesota Vikings, he elicited many exclamations of awe because of his swiftly churning legs.

He was so good that some people went overboard with a nickname, dubbing him "Purple Jesus." He was good, but certainly in the minds of many Christians, who may have found the choice of moniker objectionably irreligious, not *that* good. Purple is so strongly identified with the Vikings that part of the nickname was perfectly understandable.

———

However, "Purple Jesus" was very much team specific. Once Peterson went off to play for the New Orleans Saints, he was no longer purple. And as injuries mounted, he was no longer anyone's idea of a team savior. So "Purple Jesus" was a nickname with an expiration date.

———

Maybe it was only during the heyday of the Pittsburgh Steelers' 1970s–1980s Super Bowl runs, but reading up on old stories about Terry Bradshaw, references to the quarterback as "The Blond Bomber" did not seem common.

———

Once upon a time, the Hall of Famer out of Louisiana Tech did have blond hair. But he has been bald for so long, it's difficult to know how many football fans remember that. One can look back at Bradshaw's early football cards and view wavy blond hair, however.

———

Craig "Ironhead" Heyward's moniker seems to be self-explanatory. You didn't head-butt with the late NFL running back and expect to get away with less than a headache and possibly a concussion.

> "Heyward was apparently capable of using his noggin as a deadly force, much like professional wrestlers must have heads that can survive battles with foreign objects. Heyward had a large hat size of 8¾, so those adjustable baseball caps were just right for him."

It could have been that "Ironhead"'s body strong point was his head, although his physique of 5-foot-11 and 265 pounds might imply otherwise. One story about Heyward's hardheadedness is that someone once tried to attack him with a pool cue, but when the stick collided with Heyward's head, it broke (the pool cue, that is).

Lance Alworth was one of the greatest players in NFL saddled with one of the mushiest, lamest, too-polite nicknames of all time: Bambi. Many other players were given good, solid, scary football-type nicknames stressing their behemoth size, their toughness, or their meanness. Not Alworth. Charger teammates nicknamed him after the Walt Disney movie of the same name. A Hall of Fame receiver who ran like a deer, with long legs, speed, and shiftiness, like Bambi the cartoon character, Alworth also had big brown eyes. While his teammates noted that, today it might only be used as a selling point on match.com.

They named Alworth after Bambi. Yep, the fragile, baby deer that must dodge hunters (defenders?) before becoming Great Prince of the Forest. Was this actually a compliment? Maybe, sorta. But the movie, which came out in 1942, and the connection to Alworth, has proven durable and memorable. And also pretty weird.

PRO HOCKEY PLAYERS

In many cases, the basic idea of nicknames may be weird. Other times, they are bland and routine. But sometimes a doozy stands out. Sometimes a name that was once thought to be unusual may have been repeated so many times, everyone got used to it.

Baseball used to be the real sport of nicknames. Back in the first two-thirds of the 20th century, diamond-related nicknames were very common. Not as much these days. Hockey nicknames somehow got off track, and for some reason, just about every hockey player is called by a diminutive that ends in an "ey" sound. They're all like "Chewy" for Chewbacca in "Star Wars." Apparently, everyone who skates in the National Hockey League who wasn't named Bobby or Johnny by his parents is making up for it.

> There are some hockey player nicknames that are farther out, but some are so fundamental, you figure the kid was given it at birth and brought it with him into the NHL.

There are some weird ones, some good ones, and not so good ones. For good reason, Wayne Gretzky is called "The Great One," but more cynically, his brother Brent is called "The Not So Great One," because he wasn't nearly as good a player as Wayne. Johnny Gaudreau was called Johnny Hockey. That sounds cool, if more like a gangster than a skater. David Backes was called "Captain America" because he was a 2-time Olympian for the United States, not because he carried a shield. One of goalie Ed Belfour's nicknames was "Eddie the Billionaire." Belfour did well for himself, but he definitely didn't earn a billion dollars playing hockey.

Jordie Benn wears a big, fat beard. So does a stuffed character named Yukon Cornelius, a pistol-packing lumberjack-looking guy, who appeared in a 1970s Christmas movie *Rudolph The Red-Nosed Reindeer*. It is no surprise Benn acquired that nickname, although few NHL players tote around stuffed animals. A few years ago, the Minnesota Wild, playing against Benn's Dallas Stars, sought to make fun of him by throwing a picture of Yukon Cornelius on its big screen arena videoboard. Only Benn loved it.

Likely more players would prefer to be called Yukon Cornelius than "The Norwegian Hobbit Wizard," as was pinned on Mats Zuccarello, a player from Norway. Is it a good thing or a bad thing to be nicknamed "Gorilla," as was Niclas Wallin of Sweden? Weirdly, but understandably, Marc-Edouard Vlasic was called "Pickles," since his last name is the same as that of a product manufacturer.

It does not translate glibly out of context, but Georges Vezina, for whom the famed goaltending award was named, was nicknamed "The Chicoutimi Cucumber." That combined the name of his hometown in Quebec with a description of how coolly Vezina protected the goalmouth. Quite obvious as a choice, Tomas Tatar had to put up with the nickname "Tatar Sauce." One step removed and one step cleverer was the backup nickname of Hot Sauce.

> Max Bentley, one of 6 hockey-playing brothers, was called "The Dipsy-Doodle-Dandy." His offensive prowess, as exemplified by the showy nickname, got him into the Hall of Fame.

Nels Stewart, a Hall of Famer who played in the NHL in the 1920s, was called "Old Poison." He was not very old at the time he acquired the nickname, and the way he poisoned opponents was by frequent scoring, so the combination of man and nickname tilts to the weird side.

A sign reading "Rotisserie chicken, you're my favorite" has been seen in the locker room dressing stall of Nick Bjugstad of the Florida Panthers. One night, when Bjugstad was supposed to meet teammates for dinner, he couldn't find a parking place near the restaurant and decided he would hit a supermarket instead. He bought a rotisserie chicken and took it home. The guys retaliated by putting rotisserie chicken signs in his locker and talking it up in TV interviews, which prompted the creation of some fan signs. One game, Bjugstad, who apparently does not savor rotisserie chicken more than many other dishes, watched as a chicken wing was hurled onto the ice by a fan. Anyway, he got stuck with the nickname.

Gordon Berenson was always better known in the sport as "Red," as many red-haired athletes are. His given name was bestowed in honor of the great Gordie Howe. Berenson's expanded nickname was "The Red Baron," not to honor the World War I German flying ace (who was also Snoopy's nemesis in the *Peanuts* comic strip), but because he flew down the ice and scored a lot of goals, including six in one game.

The great Hall of Fame netminder Johnny Bower was nicknamed "The China Wall," even though he didn't visit China and China had virtually nothing to do with hockey during his lifetime. Most famous for his term with the Toronto Maple Leafs, the over-aged achiever seemed to have a few things in common with the Great Wall of China. They were both said to be solid and old.

Eddie Dorohoy, whose NHL career lasted just 16 games with Montreal during the 1948–49 season, was a blabbermouth before his time, when rookies were supposed to be seen and not heard. He gained the nickname "The Great Gabbo" after a movie character of the 1920s who was a ventriloquist. Like many skaters, Dorohoy wanted to play more and said so in various ways. The coach criticized Dorohoy for not scoring, to which he responded, "I've been trying to score from too sharp an angle—the end of the bench."

One might say that defenseman Niklas Hjalmarsson's nickname, "Swedish Missile Defense System," is an unwieldy one, though it does include his heritage.

> Bill Juzda hit very hard in football, and the skill translated to hockey when he shifted to the ice. Rugged body checks did not earn him his nickname of "The Honest Brakeman," though. At a time in the 1940s and 1950s when pros did not make much money, Juzda supplemented his income by working on the railroad.

Patrick Kane, star of the Chicago Blackhawks and an Olympic representative of the United States, has had at least 11 nicknames bestowed on him, more than just about anyone in professional sports history. Among them are "Pattycakes," "Lil' Peekaboo," the simple "Kaner," and the little more sophisticated and cleverer "He Came He Saw He Kanequered."

David Krejci is Czech, yet his nickname is "French Fries." That is not because he is addicted to the thinly sliced potatoes. One day, he was talking about his ambition in hockey with Tyler Seguin of the Dallas Stars and said how he wanted to be viewed as the Boston Bruins' franchise player. Seguin could not understand what Krejci was saying because of his thick accent speaking English, and *franchise* got turned into *French fries*.

Hall of Famer Mark Messier collected his own assortment of nicknames. Viewed through different lenses, one could see how he acquired them. One of them was "Moose," because Messier was a big, tough guy on the ice. Another was "The Captain," because he earned that rank and was respected by teammates. Another was "Satan," presumably because he was the devil to opponents. Then there was "The Messiah," which may have been a tad sacrilegious, but if you had gone 54 seasons without a Stanley Cup championship before Messier led the Rangers to a title, you might think that way, too.

Shayne Gostisbehere, who grew up in Florida with US and French dual citizenship, was christened "Ghost Bear" after joining the Philadelphia Flyers, not because he dreamed of a dead grizzly, but because that's how people pronounced his last name. When he signed autographs, Gotisbehere included little sketches of ghosts and bears. He turned the situation into something special by creating a Ghost Bear Foundation to benefit ill or disabled children and endangered or at-risk animals.

MAJOR LEAGUE BASEBALL TEAMS

The names of many professional big-league sports teams make perfect sense. Some are based on the geography of the franchise. Some are based on a particular local trait. Many of the ingrained names have been with us for decades, or even more than a century when it comes to Major League Baseball.

However, some of those very popular names were bestowed when the teams were located in other cities. They were location specific at the time, but with the passage of time, and especially in cases where the club has moved to a new city, the nicknames no longer make all that much sense. Yet they persist, because management is loath to tamper with a name that has a public following.

The Los Angeles National League baseball team is called the Dodgers. Fans are passionate about the Dodgers. But how many of them know the origins of the nickname? It goes back to the days before 1958, when the team was situated in Brooklyn, New York. From 1895 into the 1930s, one of the Dodgers' nicknames was the Trolley Dodgers, named after fans who were adept at evading the newfangled trolleys created for public transportation.

> There are no trolleys near Chavez Ravine in Southern California, the bastion of the automobile.

By fan vote in 1995, the Arizona Diamondbacks were named after rattlesnakes, something that doesn't seem all that appealing. It could have made for the world's tallest and skinniest mascot—no one on a diet need apply.

The Chicago Cubs, founded in 1876, were one of the original National League teams. Over their early years, they went through a series of names, including the White Stockings. Of course, the American League Chicago team later took White Sox. Perhaps the weirdest nickname the Cubs had before they stuck with the Cubs was the Orphans.

The 1962 expansion team known as the Houston Colt .45s changed its name to Astros a few years later. Since Houston was a major base of action in the nation's pursuit of exploration of outer space, it seemed to make sense to be loosely affiliated with astronauts. The team also played in the Astrodome and on an artificial playing surface that was called AstroTurf.

> New York's National League team, the Mets, came into the league at the same time as Houston. The actual name of the club is the Metropolitans, but it is practically never used in conversation, in broadcasts, or in game reports.

As famous as the nickname is, the New York Yankees are really named for nothing. Previously, in the first decade of the 20th century, they were the Highlanders. The change was prompted by a newspaperman who went for Yanks because it fit into headlines easier. It sounded fairly patriotic, too, especially around the time of World War I.

Similarly, the Philadelphia Phillies aren't named for anything, either. They were born as the Philadelphia Quakers but gave that up ages ago. They were referred to as the Philadelphias for a bit, but the Philadelphia Philadelphias didn't cut it, although there are Phillies brand cigars.

There is essentially a subcategory for religion. It must be pointed out that the St. Louis Cardinals are *not* connected to the Catholic Church, but *cardinal* refers to a shade of red. The San Diego Padres *are* connected to the church, since *padre* is Spanish for priest, though the team said the name choice stems from the community being the first mission city. The club has a friar as a mascot. As for the Tampa Bay Rays, who were originally the Devil Rays, religious people protested the name choice even though it referred to the manta ray fish. It was shortened to Rays and said to represent a ray of sunshine.

NBA & ABA TEAMS

When it comes to looking for weirdness in the names of National Basketball Association teams, you've got to start with the Utah Jazz. Of course, this is a remnant from the days when the Salt Lake City-based squad represented New Orleans. New Orleans Jazz, great name. Utah Jazz, ah, not so much.

The iconic Los Angeles Lakers have a nickname that makes no sense based on geography. Los Angeles is located on the Pacific Ocean. The city is not known for its lakes. However, the previous home of the Lakers is. That would be Minnesota, known as the land of 10,000 lakes. The Lakers got their start in Minneapolis and were the NBA's first dynasty. It still seems peculiar that the Lakers took the nickname with them when they departed for the West Coast in 1960.

Hawks really have nothing to do with Atlanta. In the earliest days of the NBA, there was a team called the Tri-City Blackhawks, representing Moline and Rock Island, Illinois, and Davenport, Iowa. Red Auerbach, the famous Hall of Famer, coached the team one year. Then the team moved to Milwaukee and became the Hawks and then on to St. Louis, where behind Bob Petit, Cliff Hagan, and Clyde Lovellette, it became a powerhouse. In 1965, the franchise moved to Atlanta (still the Hawks), whether there was any local fondness for the bird or not.

What is an Indiana Pacer? It is not flora or fowl with a special connection to the Hoosier State. It is not someone who walks really fast. Sounds pretty odd on the surface. However, the Pacers' nickname derived from a somewhat logical source. The Pacers are in this way linked to the Indianapolis 500, one of the state's defining events, which of course begins led by a pace car.

In the 1960s, the American Basketball Association was formed to compete with the NBA. Although it did not reach the same overall level as the best league in the world, there were numerous successes, including all-star players who became all-time greats like "Dr. J," Julius Erving, and teams that eventually were absorbed by the NBA, including the Pacers.

> Some teams did not last long at all, but they did briefly and proudly wear colors and nicknames that were offbeat. Who can forget the Anaheim Amigos? Apparently, most people who are not trivia buffs. They were just friendly guys during their lone 1967–68 season before exiting Anaheim and becoming the Los Angeles Stars.

One superweird team nickname was the Dallas Chapparals. Walk down any street in America and ask random pedestrians what a Chapparal is, and you won't get the right answer. Some may guess it is the formal name for the leggings cowboys wear while riding bulls. Some may guess it is an endangered species in the Everglades.

The team was actually named for the Chapparal Club, the room the owners were meeting in at the Dallas Sheraton. Seriously. Quickly enough, the Chapparals became the San Antonio Spurs. You may have heard of them.

The Memphis Tams? This was a basketball team named after a hat. The nickname was based on a somewhat floppy tam-o'-shan- ter hat that was colored green, white, and gold. This was not a baseball cap by any means. It was probably very popular to wear on St. Patrick's Day, but less so on the other 364 days of the year. The Memphis basketball team had that name for 2 seasons. As the name for a team, Tams just did not roll off the tongue. That was especially true when the team played poorly enough to require Tums.

CFL & NFL TEAMS

The Toronto Argonauts are the paragons of the Canadian Football League. Founded in 1883 and the oldest professional sports fran- chise in North America that kept its original nickname (unlike the

Chicago Cubs and Philadelphia Phillies), the Argonauts were an offshoot of the Argonaut Rowing Club.

> So, the Argonaut nickname came naturally. The Rowing Club owned the football team for 83 years. All of which is interesting history but doesn't tell the modern sports fan what the heck an Argonaut is, though some may guess it is a precious metal.

Argonauts are a kind of octopus, and that sounds kind of creepy. The other option sounds much better. The Argonauts of Greek mythology were sailor-warriors who backed Jason around 1300 B.C., when he went in search of the Golden Fleece, a symbol of authority and royalty. This was definitely a much better version to adopt for a football team.

The Winnipeg Blue Bombers sounds like a pretty cool nickname. Up until 1935, the group was merely called the Winnipegs, so some enhancement was overdue. It came in the form of a sportswriter who played off of "The Brown Bomber" nickname affixed to heavyweight boxing champion Joe Louis.

It has often been said that the NFL has no sense of humor, and glancing at the nicknames displayed by the present-day franchises, one might have to agree. The nicknames are all well established in their communities and in the league, but really there is a shortage of weirdness. Most of the nicknames relate to an historical event, an industry, or some somewhat obvious characteristic that is native to the teams' areas.

Not so for the Arizona Cardinals, however. The actual cardinal, the bird, barely makes it to the state, usually inhabiting the southeastern region. The football team has covered nearly as much territory. The club is one of the oldest in the NFL, just not living in Arizona.

The Cardinals were founded as the Chicago Cardinals in 1920 and lasted there through 1959. The team up and moved to St. Louis, where there were already baseball Cardinals playing ball, and stayed there from 1960 to 1987. Then the club shifted to the Phoenix area, beginning with the 1988 season.

Going back to 1898, the team had roots in a Chicago-area athletic club. In 1901, the club moved to a different part of town and was referred to as Racine because of the street address. The owner bought old uniforms from the University of Chicago, which had maroon jerseys. By the time the hand-me-downs reached the boss, they were well-worn. The owner declared they were not maroon, but cardinal red. Hence, the Cardinals.

NHL & WHA TEAMS

When the Colorado Rockies (not to be confused with the Major League Baseball team of the same name) moved to New Jersey, a new nickname was warranted. Rockies was a nickname wisely left behind, to be assumed by the baseball team. When the New Jersey owners selected Devils as a nickname, much like the Tampa Bay baseball people, they heard from religious folk who couldn't abide it.

These were not supposed to be the red-devil Satans anyway. Akin to the story of the Loch Ness Monster, the New Jersey Pine Barrens forest had long been said to be home of the Jersey Devil. This was alleged to be a flying creature with hooves sighted about as often as Bigfoot.

Unless a local zoo has a colony, Pittsburgh does not have any Penguins. They are not native to the neighborhood. But the jersey logo is great, the name is beloved, and it works. It was dreamed up as the choice by the owner's wife for two reasons. Penguin started with a *P*, and the nickname of the Civic Arena was The Big Igloo. Never mind that igloos are associated with Alaskan Eskimos and penguins hang out in Antarctica, in the other direction.

> The venerable Boston Bruins may associate the word Bruin with bears, but a long-time-ago owner also owned a grocery store chain that had colors of yellow and brown. The team nickname had to fit in.

It seems somewhat strange that a team would wish to commemorate terrible disasters with a feel-good entertainment enterprise, but that's how the Carolina Hurricanes got their nickname. Previously, the team was the New England Whalers, which was a darned logical nickname with proud historical roots.

By the same token, the Tampa Bay Lightning received its nickname due to a ratcheted down meteorological phenomenon—a thunderstorm.

In 1971, an archeological find near Nashville, Tennessee, produced a saber-toothed tiger. Later, when professional hockey came to town, the club was nicknamed the Predators in the long-deceased tiger's honor.

Speaking of reminding fans of disaster, the Calgary Flames, which had every chance to start over when the team moved from Atlanta, for some reason chose to stick with Flames. This name made sense when the team was based in Atlanta, because it referred to an historical event, Union General William Sherman's scorched-earth march to the sea during the Civil War. Logical, yes, but why would you want to remember that every day in game stories?

Likely no one who resides outside of Canada actually knows what the Vancouver Canucks' nickname is based on. It's a good one, going back to 1869. During that time period, there was a political cartoon character named Johnny Canuck. Johnny made a comeback during World War II as a figure who battled against the bad guys. Also, Canuck is a generic term for Canadian.

Perhaps weirdest of all was the Anaheim Mighty Ducks. The nickname was inspired by a Walt Disney hockey movie of the same name. Later, after the Disney company sold the team, the nickname was shortened to Ducks. That really isn't much better, especially if one can envision an entire arena quacking in support of an on-ice rush.

The San Jose Sharks' nickname itself isn't weird, since the city is not far from the ocean where many kinds of sharks live. However, as did many other newer teams, management provided a list of finalist choices for fans to vote on. It was a good thing Sharks came out on top, because who would want to be named the Rubber Puckies or the Screaming Squids, 2 other finalists?

In the early 1970s, the National Hockey League faced a challenge from the new World Hockey Association. Creation of the league was announced in 1971, and play began in 1972. Almost amazingly, none of the first teams had a weird nickname. The Miami Screaming Eagles were borderline unusual, but somewhat catchy.

During the league's existence, there really was no outstanding weirdly named team, although the Minnesota Fighting Saints and the Toronto Toros made bids. Well, there were the Cincinnati Stingers, which took their nickname from bumblebees.

MINOR LEAGUE BASEBALL TEAMS

Some decades in the past, most minor league baseball teams were identified by the same nickname as their parent club, so teams at every level of the minors would also be the Red Sox or something like that. There were always outliers, teams owned by the community and not affiliated with a big-league club, and they tended to have their own heritage and names. Basically, it is not weird if a team in the minors borrows the name of a team in the majors. But there are some juicy ones out there that have nicknames stemming from independent thinking. You gotta love those.

In some cases, it is obvious the owners of the teams wanted to be different and provide flavor in the nicknames for their fans.

Over the years, Albuquerque, New Mexico, has had various minor league teams, but the current one is named the Isotopes. Isotopes are atoms that have the same number of protons in their atomic nuclei. And that takes baseball analytics further than a fan ever wanted it to go.

> Strangely, this was not made up by associates of the team, but taken from *The Simpsons* cartoon show, which occasionally featured a fake team of that name. Now the Isotopes are a Triple A club associated with the Colorado Rockies.

The Pensacola Blue Wahoos are the AA franchise connected to the Cincinnati Reds. The name came from an idea submitted by a fan before the team began play in this location on Florida's Gulf Coast in 2012.

Wahoos are fish that can grow to be more than 8 feet long and weigh more than 180 pounds. They thrive in warm waters, and they are wicked fast. These fish can swim up to 60 mph, which is lightning quick in the ocean, and they have sharp teeth. Apparently, all of the traits you want in a baseball team, including a built-in cheer of "Wahoo!" when the hometown guy hits a home run.

Another AA team in Florida is the Jacksonville Jumbo Shrimp. That doesn't even sound real, but it is. Ask the Miami Marlins. That's the parent team. If players showboat, is that like dipping shrimp in too much cocktail sauce? This Jacksonville team was well known for many years as the Suns, and fans were irked when a new owner slapped this nickname on the team.

The current logo is of a Jumbo Shrimp being angry. Maybe that's because when you order shrimp in a restaurant, most of the time the heads are cut off.

El Paso, Texas, has seen minor-league baseball come and go. When it came back in 2013, the patrons were blessed with a new nickname for a team, indeed, an unprecedented nickname for a team. The San Diego Padres' AAA affiliate is called the El Paso Chihuahuas. You have never seen anything until you take a gander at the ticked-off little dog that is pictured on the team logo. It's hard to keep from laughing at the angry, snarling animal. (Maybe they feed it jumbo shrimp.)

The Richmond Flying Squirrels are the AA minor-league outfit linked to the San Francisco Giants in Virginia. The team itself played under many other guises in the Northeast. It was dubbed the Flying Squirrels through a locally organized contest.

Although not explicitly stated, one would hope the inspiration for this name is Rocky the Flying Squirrel from the 1959–1964 legendary cartoon series called *Rocky and His Friends*. If it is not, it makes no sense whatsoever.

That conclusion seems to be true, since the team has 2 Flying Squirrel Mascots, one named Nutzy, and the other Nutasha. Neither in the slightest way resembles Rocky, who was cool-looking with the aviator's cap and pilot's glasses adorning his head.

It's not even easy to explain the New Orleans Baby Cakes nickname. While there has been baseball in New Orleans for ages, it was only recently that the team began calling itself the Baby Cakes. Baby cakes is the kind of a comment that could get a masher slapped across the face in a bar anywhere but New Orleans apparently.

Baby Cakes are actual cakes, also called King Cakes, sugary bread with multicolored frosting. Going way, way back, supposedly the 3 kings brought this gift to Baby Jesus on the 12th day of Christmas. More recently, the cakes are commonly seen during Mardi Gras. There was a time when plastic toy babies were associated with baby cakes, but now the team emblem actually is a slugging baby wearing a crown.

It's a reasonably dense story with different interpretations at different times through history, but no one can deny Baby Cakes is a weird name for a minor-league baseball team.

ABOUT THE AUTHOR

L ew Freedman is a veteran newspaper sportswriter for the *Philadelphia Inquirer*, *Chicago Tribune*, and *Anchorage Daily News*. He currently writes for the *Cody Enterprise* in Wyoming.

———

Freedman is the author of more than 100 books, mostly about sports, and is constantly on the lookout for games' weird happenings and oddities.

SOURCES

BOOKS

Baseball Wit, Bill Adler, Crown Publishers, Inc., New York, New York, 1986.

Behind the Net: 101 Incredible Hockey Stories, Stan Fischler, Sports Publishing, New York, New York, 2013.

Body Slams! In Your Face Insults from The World of Pro Wrestling, Glenn Liebman, McGraw-Hill, New York, New York, 2001.

Joy in Mudville: The Big Book of Baseball Humor, Edited by Dick Schaap and Mort Gerberg, Broadway Books, New York, New York, 1982.

The Wit and Wisdom of Ozzie Guillen, Brett Ballantini, Triumph Books, Chicago, Illinois, 2006.

The Yucks! Two Years in Tampa With the Losingest Team in NFL History, Jason Vuic, Simon & Schuster, New York, New York, 2016.

Travels with Stanley, The Keepers of The Cup, Triumph Books, Chicago, Illinois, 2007.

NEWSPAPERS

Chicago Sun-Times, Mark J. Konkol, "Car Hits 'Woo-Woo,' Leaves Him with Boo-Boo," April 19, 2005.

Chicago Tribune, William Hageman, "One Day in The Life of Ronnie 'Woo-Woo' Wickers," February 27, 2004.

New York Herald-Tribune, Harold Rosenthal, "Take Me Out to Ball Game Written on Subway In '08," March 16, 1958.

WEBSITES

Bangkok.com, (No Byline) "History of Sepak Takraw" [no date].

Basketballinsiders.com, Joel Brigham, "The Dumbest NBA Injuries," July 20, 2015.

Bathdays.com, "2018 Tub Race Rules," April, 2018.

Bathtubbing.com, Loyal Nanaimo Bathtub Society. [no date].

Bleacherhideaway.com, Johnny Evers, February 5, 2008.

Bleacher Report.com, Kirby Miller, "Ranking The 25 Weirdest Sports Injuries of All Time," April 10, 2017.

Frank Passalacqua, "12 Strangest Injuries in NFL History," July 9, 2011. Nicholas Goss, "15 Oddest Injuries In NHL History," January 12, 2012. Brad Kurtzberg, "NHL: The 50

Most Gruesome Injuries in Hockey History," October 17, 2012. Marcel Smith, "NBA Legends' Funniest Quotes," October 24, 2008. Dickie Greenleaf, "The 20 Worst Team Names in Professional Sports," January 30, 2011.

Brainyquote.com, Muhammad Ali quotes, June 3, 2016. Yogi Berra, September 22, 2015.

Business Insider, Tony Manfred, "Presenting: The 20 Craziest Players in the NBA," February 21, 2012.

Buzzfeed.com, Jack Moore, "The Most WTF Sports Stories of All Time," January 23, 2013.

CBS Sports, Cody Benjamin, "Cooper's Hill Cheese-Rolling and Wake: Some Dude Tore His Calf Muscle to Set A New Cheese-Chasing Record," May 30, 2018.

CNN.com, Neil Curry, "Cotswolds Olimpicks: Shin-Kicking at the 'Other' Games," June 9, 2012.

Capoeirabrasil.com [No Byline], "The History of Capoeira" [no date].

dujuor.com. (Du Jour Magazine), Lindsay Silverman, "Rodman's Revelations, Dennis Rodman Opens Up About North Korea And Kim Jong-Un," May, 2014.

ESPN.com, Arash Markazi, "USC's Josh Shaw Admits to Lying," August 27, 2014.

Tim MacMahon, "Blazers Find Snake in Locker Room," May 8, 2014.

Fox News, Ryan Gaydos, "Former WWE Superstar Appears to Wrestle Away GOP Nomination in Tennessee Mayoral Race," May 2, 2018.

Fox Sports, Dieter Kurtenbach, "Trevor Bauer And the Most Ridiculous Injuries in Baseball History," October 20, 2016.

ftw.usatoday.com, Charles Curtis, "The 10 Weirdest Baseball Team Names (Ranked), March 31, 2017. Chris Chase, "Strange-But-True Origin Stories Of 19 Sports Team Names," February 9, 2015. Nate Scott, "The 50 Greatest Yogi Berra Quotes," September 23, 2015. Nick Schwartz, "The U. K's Cheese Rolling Contest Is Carnage," May 29, 2018.

gq.com, Alex Wong, "The 73 Hilarious, Savage and Absurd Quotes That Have Defined the NBA Season (So Far)," February 11, 2016.

Goturkeytourism.com [no byline], "Traditional Camel Wrestling Sport" [no date].

Hockeygods.com [no byline], "Unicycle Hockey" [no date].

Huffington Post.com, Kyli Singh, "10 Weirdest Sports You've Probably Never Heard Of," December 28, 2016. [no byline], "Ostrich Racing: One of Florida's Oddest, Oldest Attractions," May 20, 2013.

Independent.uk.co, Sophie Robehmed, "Do the Participants of Turkey's Annual Camel Wrestling Festival Enjoy It as Much as The Audience?" January 16, 2014. Dolly Dhingra, "Jolly Hockey Tricks: Unicycle Hockey Is Neither About Playing the Fool, Nor About Getting Covered in Bruises," January 31, 1994.

Kompster.com [no byline], "The Ten Rules of Shin Kicking" [no date].

MLB.com, David Adler and Manny Randhawa, "Strange but True, Freak Injuries Fairly Common," March 28, 2018.

Men's journal.com, Dan Israeli, "8 Weirdest Sporting Events to Watch Before You Die" [no date].

Mentalfloss.com, Ethan Trex, "19 Sports Injuries Weirder Than Nate Burleson's," September 25, 2013. Scott Allen, "25 Rejected Nicknames for Pro Sports Teams," May 29, 2015. Ransom Riggs, "Gurning: The 800-Year-Old Face-Making Competition," March 4, 2010.

Myactivesg.com [no byline], "Rules and Regulations of Sepak Takraw" [no date].

Myswitzerland.com [no byline], "Hornussen: Where the Nouss Flies from The Ramp and Into the Playing Field" [no date].

News.com.au/travel [no byline], "Dineka Maguire Wins World Bog Snorkelling Championships in Waen Ryyd Bog, Wales," August 26, 2013.

NewYorkTimes.com, Pam Bullock, "Get Out Your Boards: Extreme Ironing May Soon Be Hot," May 21, 2004.

Quoteinvestigator.com [no byline], (Tallulah Bankhead/Willie Mays), February 7, 2016.

Ranker.com, Blake Edwards, "Athletes Who Suffered the Most Bizarre Off-Field Injuries" [no date].

Reuters.com [no byline], "Lithuanian Couple Win World Wife-Carrying Championship in Finland," July 7, 2018.

SB Nation, Jon Bois, "The 35 Best Sports Tweets in Twitter History (A Painfully Subjective Roundup)," March 21, 2016. James Brady, "Nathan's Hot Dog Eating Contest 2017 Results: Joey Chestnut Wins 10th Title," July 4, 2017.

SI.com, Brendan Maloy, "The Weirdest Minor League Baseball Team Names, (Ranked)," February 26, 2016. Michael McKinley, "Bathtub Racing Can Be Good, Clean Fun," May 11, 1987.

Seeker.com/bogsnorkelers, Alyssa Danigelis, "Bog Snorkelers Compete in Wales for Mucky Glory," September 7, 2016. [no byline] "What Is Zorbing? And Is It Really Fun If You're Over 20?" November 15, 2011.

Smithsonianmag.com, Juan Golcalves-Borrega, "How Brazilian Copeira Evolved from A Martial Art on An International Dance Craze," September 21, 2017.

SportsGazette.co.uk, Will Pearse, "Inside the Unusual Sport of Gurning," May 2, 2018.

Sports.net.ca/hockey, Luke Fox, "10 Craziest All-Time, Non-Hockey NHL Injuries," January 10, 2012.

Sportsonearth.com, Asher Kohn, "The Art of Camel Wrestling," March 6, 2014.

Swissinfo.ca/eng [no byline] "Out and About in Switzerland: Anyone for Hornussen?" August 17, 2000.

Telegraph.uk.co/news, Harry Alsop, "Sumo Wrestlers Bring Babies to Tears at Japan's Nakizumo Festival," April 27, 2014. Paul Harris, "Zorbing Was the Scariest 30 Seconds of My Life," July 30, 2015.

The Guardian.com [no byline], "Gloucestershire Cheese Winner Is the All-Time Grate," May 28, 2018. Sam Murphy, "All You Need to Know About: Capoeira," March 16, 2007.

Thestar.com/sports, Jordan Winnett, "Unicyle Hockey Starting to Take Off in United Kingdom," May 17, 2013.

Thesportster.com/entertainment, William Johnston, "Top 20 Bizarre Incidents in Sports History," March 2, 2015. Johnny Hughes, "Top 15 Weirdest Injuries in Sports History," April 20, 2015.

Thesun.co.uk. /archives/news, Shakeel Hashim, "Ostrich Racing Is Real . . . With Actual Jockeys and Terrifying Breakneck Speeds," March 15, 2016.

Tofugo.com, Koichi, "Showa Shinzan Yukigassen Tournament: The World's Scariest Snowball Fight?" February 2, 2015

Topendsports.com [no byline], "Bog Snorkeling" [no date]. [no byline], "Ostrich Racing" [no date].

Travelandleisure.com, Melissa Locker, "In Japan Snowball Fighting Is A Sport Called Yukigassen," February 5, 2016.

Upc-online.org, ostriches, [no byline, *Arizona Republic*], "A Brief History Of The Chandler Ostrich Festival," March 15, 2017.

Yukigassen-intl.com [no byline], "What's Yukigassen?" [no date].

Zorbingtime.com [no byline], "Zorbing – What It Is and Why It Is Awesome" [no date].

VIDEO

YouTube, July 4, 2017, "Nathan's Hot Dog Eating Contest Held in Coney Island." April 14, 2016, "25 Insane Examples of Extreme Ironing." September 14, 2017, "Sumo Wrestlers Make Babies Cry at Naki Sumo Festival."